D0952249

PERSONAL STRATEGIES
FOR REINVENTING
THE LIFE YOU WANT

GETTING THE
RIGHT
THINGS RIGHT

CHARLIE HEDGES

MULTNOMAH BOOKS · SISTERS, OREGON

GETTING THE RIGHT THINGS RIGHT
published by Multnomah Books
a part of the Questar publishing family

© 1996 by Charlie Hedges

International Standard Book Number: 0-88070-896-4

Cover illustration by Antar Dayal

Cover design by David Carlson

Printed in the United States of America

Most Scripture quotations are from:
The Holy Bible, New International Version (NIV)
© 1973, 1984 by International Bible Society,
used by permission of Zondervan Publishing House

Also quoted:
New American Standard Bible (NASB)
© 1960, 1977 by the Lockman Foundation

The Living Bible (TLB) © 1971 by Tyndale House Publishers

For information:
QUESTAR PUBLISHERS, INC.
POST OFFICE BOX 1720
SISTERS, OREGON 97759

96 97 98 99 00 01 02 03 — 10 9 8 7 6 5 4 3 2 1

For Austin.
Until you, your mom and I knew love only partly.
May we be given grace to model what is written here.

CONTENTS

ACKNOWLEDGMENTS

Every now and then your path crosses that of another person who truly understands — one who seems to grasp, almost intuitively, those passions that simmer in the cauldrons of your soul. When one comes along, it's like finding a treasure hidden. Finding five is a Godsend.

For that reason, I thank God: For Tom Thompson, who sat with me in my garden in October of 1994, listened to my wild ideas, and with a tiny glow in his eye said, "Charlie, I think we have something here." For Heather Harpham, who was the first to really, and I mean really, catch it. So much so that as senior project editor, she embraced with fervor her role as collaborator, co-creator, and constant encourager. For David Kopp, who saw the possibility and was bold enough to take the risk, and who also surprised me with insightful clarity about myself and this project. For Carol Bartley, the rock, who gave both brilliance in editing and unceasing friendship. And finally for Pam, who understands me like no other, whose belief in me and whose love strengthen me every day. May your tribes increase. The world is a better place for all of you.

Many thanks also to Lisa Schmidt for her willingness to review and critique manuscripts. And for Dr. Gerry Breshears for attempting to keep my jots jotted and my tittles titillating in chapter eleven.

THE LIFE YOU
REALLY WANT

C ould one question change the rest of your life?
It did for John Sculley.

In 1983, while standing atop a thirty-story building in New York City, Sculley, forty-two-year-old
president of Pepsi Cola, didn't realize he was about
to be asked a question that would change his life forever.

John Sculley was a riser who had moved through the ranks and
up the ladder of success at PepsiCo faster than anyone, ever. He had
joined the company in 1967, and in just seven years, at the age of
thirty-four, he became president of Pepsi Cola. In 1973 his picture
was on the cover of *Newsweek* magazine, and he found himself
quoted regularly by all the highly regarded business journals. It
would seem he had "arrived."

In the early eighties, Steve Jobs, the creative genius behind an
almost unknown company called Apple Computer, approached
Sculley with a radical idea. Jobs had decided that Sculley was the
ideal executive to take Apple to the next level. His only problem was
convincing Sculley. After several months of friendship building and

unsuccessful wooing, a frustrated Jobs made his last-ditch appeal. On the penthouse floor of a New York City high-rise, Steve Jobs asked John Sculley the question that would change his life: *"John, do you want to spend the rest of your life selling sugared water, or do you want a chance to change the world?"*

Sculley was never the same. A short time later, to the shock of many, he resigned his position at Pepsi and became CEO of Apple Computer.

Every time I read the question asked of Sculley I get goose bumps. I bet you do too. That could be because every day we hear that same kind of question — only it's not being asked by Steve Jobs, or anyone else. We're asking it of ourselves. An inner voice — sometimes whispering, sometimes shouting — questions, "Am I really doing what I want to do? How can I live a more significant life?"

HERE'S A TEST

Question #1: Imagine you are ninety years old and have lived a full life. What would you like to have accomplished in your lifetime?

Question #2: What are you doing today to make it happen?

Is there a huge chasm between who you want to be and what you are currently doing to get there? If so, don't feel bad. Over the past decade I've asked hundreds of people these same two questions, always with similar results. It seems we are too busy with daily demands to have time to do the things we feel are most important in life. As a result, we're not convinced we're getting the *right* things right.

Businesses all over the world are spending millions of dollars every year creating viable strategic plans which identify the nature of their business, their market, and their core competencies. As individuals, we too would benefit enormously by adopting a similar strategy.

I'm a facilitator for corporations. I've traveled all over the world to work with people whose particular expertise is always far superior to mine but who have gotten caught up in the clutter of it all. My job is to help them see through this chaos. In *Leadership Is an Art*, Max Depree writes, "Leaders are obligated to provide and maintain momentum.... Momentum comes from a *clear vision* of what the corporation ought to be, from a *well-thought-out strategy to achieve that vision...*" (emphasis added). When I work with corporations, I assist them in creating a clear vision and a clear plan.

I'll do the same thing with you in this book by introducing you to fresh ideas, innovative strategies, biblical truths, and even some "unreasonable thinking." I will help you reinvent the life you really want. I won't, however, tell you what your destiny should be. Who knows that better than you and God?

Perhaps you're skeptical. You should be. We are bombarded daily with marketing campaigns designed to convince us of the powerful changes we could make in our lives — if only we would subscribe to the newest technique, tool, or philosophy. Admittedly, some of these approaches are quite helpful. But many of them fall short of what we desire.

Perhaps what we really need is *not* something new, but something old. All of the "right things" discussed in the following pages are timeless, basic truths. Each can be found, in one form or another, in a book packed with wisdom and insight — the Bible. That doesn't necessarily mean these right ideas are simple or easy, but it does indicate that we're heading in the right direction.

Reinventing the life we want is an utterly pragmatic task, based on real-life scenarios and real-life experiences. But it is a profoundly spiritual task as well. It calls for us to align ourselves with creation intent. Sometimes the life we think we want (which is often the life we reach for without thinking) isn't the life we truly long for. The life we desire deep in our being is the one we were *created* to have, consistent with the way God made us. That's where we'll find the kind of significance we're after.

CONSCIOUS CHOICES

When John Sculley left PepsiCo, many people thought he was nuts. As heir apparent to the chairman of the board, his future was set. He tossed aside more money and power than you and I could dream of, for the opportunity to "change the world." Sculley decided to follow his heart. But make no mistake. It was not a blind or cavalier decision based on fleeting emotion. It was strategic.

Sculley evaluated his current position, including its growth potential. He also projected what his future state might look like with

Apple Computer and what its growth potential was. Finally, he created a plan, a strategy for becoming the John Sculley he really wanted to be. He then made his choice.

In my consulting practice I've learned an important principle — the Principle of Conscious Choices. In the scope of a normal day you will have scores, maybe even hundreds, of demands placed upon you. From the unexpected early morning phone call, to traffic patterns, to eight or nine hours of work, to kids or roommates, to household responsibilities — all these external forces make regular demands on you. And typically you respond without even thinking.

The Principle of Conscious Choices suggests that you respond to more of these demands *consciously*, on purpose, in light of your personal vision. If you decide to say yes or no, it is a purposeful decision. Simply said, the principle of conscious choices asks you to take your life back from the myriad external demands and expectations that are robbing you of your life. Your choices need to begin at a high level — the "who you want to be" level — and then filter down to your everyday decisions.

You will do a lot of things in your lifetime, but in the end only a few of them will really matter. And those are the ones you will certainly want *to do right*.

Ultimately, the choice is yours.

Reinventing the Life You Want

There's a way to begin

Before you set about getting things right, first you have to see things right. In this opening section we will "get our thinking right," and we will identify the few things that really matter in our quest for reinventing the life we really want.

The paradox is indeed that new life is born out of the pains of the old.

HENRI NOUWEN
FROM REACHING OUT

The wisdom of the prudent is to give thought to their ways....

PROVERBS 14 : 8

CHAPTER ONE

A CALL TO
UNREASONABLE
THINKING

S ome time ago I was in a room with twenty-plus corporate staffers whose tenure with the company ranged
from five to twenty-five years. As an icebreaker for our
daylong session, I asked the participants to answer three
questions about themselves for the rest of the group:
Who are you? Who were you? Who do you want to be? Most notable
were the responses I heard to the third question.

Several people disclosed admirable goals such as "I want to be a
good father" and "I want to continue to grow and learn." About a
third of the group, however, candidly told their peers, "I like my job
OK, but it's not fulfilling. I want to work with kids," or "I want to help
addicts." In short, "I want a chance to *make a difference*. I want a more
significant life."

The desires of these corporate staffers are in no way unique. I've
spoken with management and workers all over the world — from
the high-rise office buildings in San Francisco to the North Sea of the

UK to the rain forest of Papua New Guinea to the deserts of Saudi Arabia. It's amazing the number of people I find who have devoted years to pursuing their "ideal life" by means of a dream career, only to fall short of what they *really* want.

You, too, want your life to make a difference. You want a chance in life to carve your own mark and leave a tiny, yet meaningful piece of yourself behind. These desires reflect a deep and soulful drive for significance that is common to all people.

Let's be very clear at the onset: The issue is not about getting a better career (although career *can* play a major role). The issue at stake goes far beyond "what people do at work" to "what people do with their lives"! It's about making a *life* that counts.

I've led a rather eclectic life. After leaving college I was in manufacturing for twelve years, then went to seminary and was a pastor for six years. Today I'm a forty-six-year-old, self-employed, management consultant, racking up frequent-flyer miles, while trying to be a good husband and father. I tend to keep busy, and as a result, over the last five years I have come to a life-changing realization: There are a lot of things I will do in my life, but in the end, only a few of them will really matter. Those will be the *right things*.

GETTING THE RIGHT STRATEGIES

An effective adage is used in management development to describe the distinctives of a good leader. It is said that while managers concentrate on *doing things right*, leaders concentrate on *doing the right things*. In business you can do hordes of things right, such as accounting, marketing, manufacturing, and customer service. But, if you do not do *the right things*, like develop the right product for the right market and get it to the customer at the right time, you'll be out of business in a heartbeat.

The same principle is true for life in general. You are probably doing scores of things right, but are they *the right things*? Are they the kinds of things that contribute to the life you really want? The goal of this book is to help you understand exactly what your right things are and then create a realistic strategy or game plan to accomplish them. In this way you will begin the exciting steps to reinventing the life you really want.

As you will soon discover, I advocate an orderly and more or less strategic approach to self-reinvention. Even the organization of this book might be considered strategic. The order of sections and chapters is intentional, important, and sequential, each depending on the previous one:

Part One: Reinventing the Life You Want — There's a way to begin
All great strategies begin with a great philosophy. Before you set about getting things right, first you have to see things right. This opening section of three chapters concentrates on trying to "get our thinking right" and is a vital piece of the puzzle.

You may be tempted to get right into the "doing" pieces. You're ready to get to it and you want action. But consider, that's what got some of us into trouble in the first place — an overemphasis on "doing" without enough time "thinking" about why and where. Remember, even the Israelites experienced forty years of preparation before entering the promised land.

Part Two: Recovering Your Inner Assets — What are you worth?
After getting our thinking right, the next step involves investigation. All business endeavors begin with a research/data gathering phase. We ask, "What information do we need to initiate a personal process of reinvention?" Any viable effort to reinvent the life we want must begin with a solid understanding of who we are by creation. From there, we can more clearly envision who we want to be, our dream.

Part Three: Revamping Your Strategies — Putting change in action
All the serious "doing" is now ready to begin. Self-reinvention almost never happens by accident (and when it does, it always happens to somebody else). It takes a purposeful and strategic approach. Three essential strategies will greatly assist the person tackling a reinventing process.

Part Four: Carving Your Mark Deep — Making moves that matter
By this point we will be soundly on the road to reinventing the life we want. But if we want to make a difference, if we want to carve a deep mark, there remain a few things yet to do. *Impact* is the key determinant for the reinvented life. We ask, "Did my life make a difference in the people and places that counted?" We talk here about making a big life even bigger.

In all of the chapters you will learn that getting the right things right is surprisingly attainable. Stories of regular people like you and me who have created a new and significant self are found throughout. But, let's be realistic. If reinventing the life we want were simple, more people would blissfully lead their ideal lives. So, what's the problem? Why don't most people live the life they want?

BLACK HOLES

Just as there are black holes in the universe, there are also black holes in daily life that suck up opportunities for significant living like a high-powered vacuum. The following "holes" are not an exhaustive list, but they identify some of the greatest threats to inventing the life you really want.

Black Hole #1: Busyness

You are busy. You are busy because life demands that you be busy. You work nine hours a day; you have appointments, friends, dates, spouses, kids, and family; you have bills to pay, laundry to pick up, a house or apartment to clean, and a yard screaming for your care. It seems as if everyone and everything want a piece of you. You're working harder and playing harder but enjoying it less because so much is demanded of you.

There's another reason you're busy, and you probably won't like to hear it. You're busy because you want to be. Because you love it.

Because "to not be busy" is more than you can bear. Someone should write a book on "Self-Esteem according to Daytimer." I can recall when I was single the pride I took in showing someone my totally filled calendar. Something about a busy schedule has perceived value, as if busyness signifies importance, and importance proves personal value.

The subtle message, then, is to keep busy. As long as you are doing something (anything), life must be OK. But the message is a lie, and it's probably killing you. When your schedule is too demanding, it will preclude any proactive behaviors that might result in living on purpose. Your busyness becomes too overwhelming, allowing only enough time to stay just as busy tomorrow as you were today, and still go almost nowhere.

Black Hole #2: Stuckness

In his latest novel, *The Lost World*, Michael Crichton describes a fascinating new theory called "the edge of chaos": "complex systems seem to strike a balance between the need for order and the imperative to change. Complex systems tend to locate themselves at a place we call the edge of chaos. We imagine the edge of chaos as a place where there is enough innovation to keep the living system vibrant, and enough stability to keep it from collapsing into anarchy. Only at the edge of chaos can complex systems flourish."

You are a highly "complex system." And, like it or not, you are at your best on *the edge of chaos* — this wonderfully contradictory tension between stability and change.

Daily you wrestle with "the need for order and the imperative to change." On the one hand, you resonate with the idea of change and all the vibrancy and excitement it offers. In some way, you see change as your hope for the future, for only through change can you implement this new self you desire.

But on the other side of this *edge of chaos* is your need for order. You cannot resist your dominating drive to create stability, comfort, and security. There are too many unknowns in life, so you want to predict and control as much as possible. You want to minimize the number of surprises. The result is you try to get comfortable with life as you know it — even when it's bad.

Therefore, the downside of your need for stability is that you get stuck in it — stuck in the stable. As long as things are predictable, even if they are bad, you will only maintain. "Stuck in the stable" is a very black hole indeed. Although it drives you crazy, it is still so comfortable. It's like a drug, and like a drug it demands detox if you wish for better things in life.

Black Hole #3: Hopelessness

When busyness and stuckness hunker down and take their full toll, you lose sight of any hope. "How can I change?" you ask. "It would require far more time and energy than I have. Besides, I've tried that before and it doesn't work." When you finally reach the point of hopelessness, the black hole seems so vast there isn't a ladder in the universe long enough to get you out. I know. I've been there. A lot.

When I was thirty-two, I was stuck in an unfulfilling job and had a burning desire to become a minister. But in order to become a minister, I needed seminary education. So I called around to find out what it would take. One local institution informed me that because of course work I had not completed in college, my seminary training would take five years.

"Five years!" I thought. "I couldn't start until next year, so I wouldn't finish until I'm thirty-eight!" My hopes were dashed.

As I was explaining my situation to a friend who had made a career change at forty, he said, "Charlie, you're going to be thirty-eight anyway. Why not be thirty-eight and doing something you enjoy?"

Don Carlson's simple comment redirected my whole thought process. All I really needed was a dose of hope. I also needed to hear from someone else who had traveled along the road I wanted to walk, someone who was familiar with the road and could encourage me a bit.

Black holes — and you could list a dozen others — suck the hope out of life. We forget what matters. Left unchallenged, black holes will prevent us from ever acting on that creative and vibrant persona with which God has so graciously endowed us. They will (and do) prevent us from being the people we want to be. Black holes, like everything else in life, must be managed. But before they can be adequately managed, we need to analyze both the problem and solution in fresh and creative ways — in ways that might even be considered "unreasonable."

UNREASONABLE AND RIGHT

We cannot get things right until we see things right. Sometimes, in order to see things right, we have to turn them on their head and look at them upside down or backwards.

In *The Age of Unreason*, a brilliant and truly prophetic book on the future of the world of work, Charles Handy argues that in today's world all progress depends on unreasonable people, ones who are less stuck in cultural paradigms. They tend to be revolutionary, grasping a need, envisioning a solution, and acting boldly to implement. Handy says, "For any change of consequence we must look to the unreasonable man or to the unreasonable woman." I agree.

Jesus was an unreasonable man.

The religious community of his time certainly thought so. Think about it. When Jesus initiated his earthly strategy, he was surrounded by experts who disagreed with him. Jesus' primary antagonists were the religious leaders, the scholarly elite. They had devoted decades to the study of Scripture and related texts. They knew them inside and out. And they thought Jesus was unreasonable.

According to the standard beliefs of his time, he was. "Reason" dictated that people follow the experts. But Jesus turned things upside down and looked at them quite differently. Consider some of his unreasonable and upside-down ideas...

When struck, turn the other cheek.
When you merely think about adultery, you're guilty.

When you slander someone, you're a murderer.
To truly live you must die.
Give away all your earthly possessions.
If someone continues to sin against you, forgive him at least
*   490 times.*
Your actions are less important than your heart.

Outrageous and unreasonable, but right! When the masses followed the words of Jesus, it was because what he said was so true. Unreasonable as it may have sounded, the moment they heard his message, they knew it was right and that it was the only way to live.

Jesus was an unreasonable man.

This book is largely about unreasonable thinking. It is not about "being unreasonable" for its own sake; rather it is a call to be genuine, to rely on an old message offered in a fresh way and to listen only to those voices that matter — the voice of your heart, the voice of those who love you, and the voice of God. It will call you to turn things upside down, look at life backwards and inside out so that in the end you will understand how reasonable it is to be unreasonable.

REINVENTION: THE ROAD TO MAKING A DIFFERENCE

Around the age of sixty-five Bill Phelps' life was turned upside down. After a number of unwanted changes in his career, family, and friends, he found he had lost much of what he held dear. Because he had always been entrepreneurial — from starting two successful companies to getting his pilot's license at the age of fifty-five — Bill was sharp enough to recognize that he needed a new direction.

Bill decided it was time to "reinvent himself" — to evaluate his talents, investigate his options, and pursue new directions, including new friendships, hobbies, and ways to feel "accomplished." One of these directions was nature photography. Since that time, Bill has traveled the United States and Canada, photographing all the national parks, and at eighty-five years old, he is still receiving national acclaim for his photography.

A reinvented life can take on innumerable faces. It may involve a change in status, such as pursuing a new career, or maybe a change in behavior, like devoting more time to the people you love. It might mean an entirely new approach to life through a profound spiritual conversion. Or maybe a reinvented life will simply call for spending more time doing the things you love.

I know scores of people, all with different needs and different stories, who have changed their lives. Fifteen years ago my friend Steve Hreha spent his workdays carrying a hundred-pound hod of plaster up and down ladders, while wishing he could break a hundred on the golf course. Steve changed himself, and today he owns his own plastering company with a half-dozen employees, and he plays to a four handicap.

For years Nancy Barna managed the office, finances, and administration of the Barna Research Group. Now that she is a mother of two, Nancy has elected to reinvent herself. She loves her kids and she loves using her brain, so today Nancy devotes the bulk of her time to her two daughters, while also maintaining a small hand in BRG operations as well as managing the corporate finances.

Reinventing the life you want is not about taking a picture of someone you admire and then recreating yourself in that person's image. It's not even about simply imagining your perfect life and then trying to accomplish it. It is about being consistent with the truest you as you grapple with who you are by creation and then living accordingly. But make no mistake, this process is a work best done in harmony with God.

THE COST OF REINVENTION

The reinventors just described are everyday, regular people, like you and me, who have found a way to live better, more meaningfully, more productively, and with greater impact and greater personal significance. Inventing a significant life is very doable. But I have to be honest with you: I cannot promise that you will have success or find your significance as a result of reading this book. Promise fulfillment is not within my bailiwick. That is wholly in the hands of you and God.

I can promise only one thing. I can promise hope, and a lot of it. Intermingled with that hope is the paradox of life: Life is difficult and unpredictable, filled with roadblocks and black holes. But life is also magnificent, filled with love and value and wonder. The paradox is that life is a difficult and unpredictable wonder. The people who have successfully reinvented their lives have learned to manage the paradox through perseverance, desire, and hard work.

When I work with corporations, my daily fees are fairly high, and apparently in my customers' eyes the value of my services is equal to my fee or I wouldn't be asked to return. On the other hand, when I work on a *pro bono* basis and offer my services for free, I find a different attitude. People show up late or offer lame excuses to leave early. Human nature is to give low value to low cost.

The cost of significance is not cheap. If it were, it wouldn't be significant.

The same is true for your pursuit of significance. Your most valued accomplishments and your most treasured possessions are the ones which required sacrifice, effort, and hard work. The cost of significance is not cheap. If it were, it wouldn't be significant.

In the words of Spinoza: "All things excellent are as difficult as they are rare."

Getting the right things right begins by thinking right things. Your process of self-reinvention begins by knowing you have great hope. It is an eminently doable process. Success stories abound. But just because it is doable, doesn't necessarily mean it will be simple. It will take work.

It will require you to call out your black holes, identify them, and fight them. It will also require you to look at things at an "unreasonable" angle, sometimes sideways, sometimes upside down. And, finally, as you will discover in the next chapter, you will have to clearly understand those *right things* which must be done.

Right Turns

RECALL THE RIGHT IDEAS

- It is possible to reinvent our lives in an intentional, planned way by learning to focus on the right things.
- Reinvented living calls for two things: "unreasonable thinking" and conscious choices.
- Our desire for significant living can be dissipated by black holes that rob us of the time and energy we need to do the things that matter.
- The search for significant living is a lot of work, but worth the effort.

DECIDE WHAT'S RIGHT FOR YOU

- Why are you reading this book?
- Make a list of what you consider the "right things" in your life.
- Recall previous attempts you've made to change your life. How successful were they? Do you know why?
- What is your biggest black hole? Why?

MAKE THE RIGHT MOVES

- Start a "Key Idea" notebook that chronicles your reactions and plans concerning each chapter of this book.

- Tell one friend what you are reading and that you plan to make changes in your life.
- Write a paragraph or two describing what you think a significant life would look and feel like.
- Resist the temptation to make lofty resolutions or to expect quick fixes.

Whether he works in business or in a hospital, in a government agency or in a labor union, in a university or in the army, the executive is, first of all, expected to get the right things done.

PETER DRUCKER
FROM *THE EFFECTIVE EXECUTIVE*

"Serve the LORD with all your heart. And you must not turn aside, for then you would go after futile things, which can not profit or deliver, because they are futile."

1 SAMUEL 12:20-21, NASB

CHAPTER TWO

THE FEW THINGS THAT MATTER

I t was a nut house. It had been that way for almost two days. Servants frantically scurried about like mice sniffing out cheese. Delivery boys came and then went as quickly, bringing food and flowers and wines and table settings and guest registers. Yet for all the precise planning chaos still prevailed. The mistresses of the manor were no better off, especially the older sister who was quite concerned with propriety. They were about to serve dinner to the most influential man in the country. Things better be perfect!

When their honored guest finally arrived, the younger sister immediately fell into that seemingly irresponsible behavior that just ticked off her sibling — she abandoned all her preparations and went into the sitting room to chat with all their guests and listen to the words of the honored one.

After a short time the older sister's frustration peaked. She charged into the sitting room and said to their guest, "Jesus, don't you care that my sister has left me to do the serving all alone? Tell her to help me!"

Jesus responded, "Martha, Martha, you are worried and bothered by so many things; but only a few things are necessary, really only one, and Mary has chosen the good part, which shall not be taken away from her."

This story, first written almost two thousand years ago, has as much relevance today as it did then. It describes a tension within almost every human being, the tension between doing things right and doing the right things.

You could say you have two sisters residing within you. One sister, Martha, is concerned about doing things right, about propriety, appearance, timeliness, and orderliness. The other sister, Mary, is the soulful one who pushes you toward a life of impact and significance. In many ways this book is about listening to your Mary. She is your leader within who is less concerned with doing things right than with doing the right things. To Mary, activity is nothing without meaning and results. Her voice asks, "Why?" "Does it really matter in the long run?" "Will it get me where I want to go?"

As I was having lunch with a young business executive, he described the problems of raising a seven-year-old daughter in an upscale community. He and his wife have faced an onslaught of peer pressure from other parents to make sure they "expose" their daughter to a whole host of developmental options. They were told she should experiment with a full set of sports, including soccer, baseball, basketball, and volleyball. She should dance, not just ballet but tap and modern as well. She definitely needed at least one foreign language, considering we live in a global village. And what about developing her computer skills? All of this was in addition to the routine expectations of her education at a private school.

"It's overwhelming," this father nearly yelled in the restaurant. "We've decided to ignore what other people are suggesting and simply show our daughter a few good things in a timely way without running the risk of making her neurotic." He observed that in America we worship a god named "choice" and a philosophy that says the more choices and options we have, the better our chance for success. Unfortunately, the god of "choice" only keeps us busy, it doesn't necessarily contribute to living a significant life.

It is possible to do a lot of things right, and still do life all wrong.

Five years ago I realized I had to adjust the focus of my attention. I had too many things going on, too many people tugging at me, too many pressures demanding my immediate attention. I was in the middle of starting a new business, trying to buy a new home, developing new training programs, wondering which, if any, of my nonfamily relationships were worth keeping, and spending too much time on airplanes, while trying to maintain some sanity.

It seemed if I could somehow refocus my attention, I would be far better off. I thought of the story of Mary and Martha and wondered what Jesus was talking about when he said to Martha, "You are worried and bothered about so many things; *but only a few things are necessary*" (NASB, emphasis mine).

SEARCHING FOR A FEW RIGHT THINGS

I have spent a lot of time wondering about those few right things that matter. What could they be? I've read widely on the subject; I've interviewed friends and clients; I've talked to pastors and rabbis. In the last three years I've observed life in eleven different countries. Shoot, I've even prayed about it. And I have collected quite a shopping list, from inner qualities like love, charity, kindness, and integrity; to achievement-oriented items such as getting ahead, accomplishments, and acquisitions; to a whole host of spiritual qualities found in worship and obedience.

I found a lot of people with a lot of ideas — but little concurrence. I began to think the whole idea of a few things that matter for life must be so centered around each individual that it would be impossible to name a generic list for all of us.

Then it hit me. Life's few right things aren't found in the things themselves, but rather in the way you arrange and organize those things. It's merely a matter of understanding the basics. Grasping this truth was the giant "aha" that propelled me to comprehend the few right things that matter.

I now believe that of all the things you can do in your life, four "right" areas or domains matter most. And if you concentrate your life on these four areas, in the end you'll be able to hold your head high as you proclaim, "My life really mattered!"

What are they? First read about them in the following story.

THE LEGEND OF AUSTIN THE GREAT

Once upon a time in a faraway kingdom there lived an energetic young knight named Austin.

Austin was great in the eyes of his young peers in the King's School of Knighthood. He was the best at archery, fencing, riding, and fighting. He consistently received the highest marks in academics. But, as a newly ordained member of the Royal Brotherhood of Knights, Austin had much yet to learn. So the older knights appointed a counselor to guide him in the ways of mature knighthood. And since Austin showed such promise, they gave him Sapientius, the wisest and most respected man on the Council of Elders.

At their first meeting Sapientius asked Austin, "Tell me, to what end do you strive?"

"That is a simple question to answer, sire," replied the not-yet-so-humble Austin. "I strive to be greatest among the knights. I strive to be Champion of the Council of Elders."

"I see," said Master Sapientius as he pondered the arduous task before him. "Let's test your worth. There is a great dragon named Dreamkiller seeking to destroy a tiny village south of the king's city. Your mission is to delay him until the army can arrive. You may take with you whomever you wish to accomplish your task."

Eager to prove himself, Austin decided not to take anyone with him on this mission. It would be far better for his reputation to do this noble task alone. Then all would revere him, and he would surely be considered great.

But things did not turn out as Austin desired. Dragons are very clever, and when Dreamkiller saw a single warrior approaching in full armor, he knew he would have his way. As Austin finally approached the dragon, he boldly announced, "Dragon, today you shall be slain!" Dreamkiller only smiled and blew a bit of smoke just to let Austin know what he was in for.

Three days later Austin returned to Sapientius, having failed his mission. The dragon was still about and the people still unprotected. "My armor and broadswords were useless against Dreamkiller," he complained. "I tried all that the teachers of battle taught me and it was to no avail. I failed."

Sapientius took Austin firmly in his grasp and told him he was now ready for his lessons in mature knighthood. "There are four things you must always remember if you are to be great. The first is 'Know Yourself.' The reason you failed your mission was that you were too busy trying to be like all the warriors you studied in school. You used their armor, their weapons, and their strategy. You failed to understand your own special gifts and talents. Did you consider using your gifts of negotiation and planning? Instead of choosing to search within yourself, you chose to be like someone else. Know yourself, my son, and you will take the first step to greatness.

"The second thing you must remember is the 'Value of Camaraderie.' A great warrior never fights wholly alone, unless he absolutely has to. You should have gathered other young knights whom you trusted. Together you could have created a plan to defeat Dreamkiller. Did you know that dragons are not only clever, but they are also vain? I imagine if one of you were to play on the dragon's vanity, the other might gain an opportunity to find the soft spot on his belly. Then you might do damage to the dragon and accomplish your mission. Austin, you must know yourself and you must also count on others."

So Austin gathered a small company of compatriots and departed to do battle with Dreamkiller. Armed with the wisdom of Sapientius, not only did the small company of young knights delay the great dragon, they utterly destroyed him. News reached the king's city, and when

Austin returned, he was hailed as a great and wonderful warrior. All the city shouted his name and sang songs of his unparalleled glory. Austin, at a very young age, had accomplished his goal. He was the greatest among the king's warriors.

It was several days before he met again with Sapientius. At their encounter Austin dropped to his knees and said to his teacher, "Thank you, sire. For through your wisdom I have attained my desire. I have slain Dreamkiller, and I am revered as the greatest of all the king's knights."

Sapientius was saddened by the comments of his young prodigy. "You still have far to go, my son, if you truly wish to be great. For the person of greatness seeks not greatness solely for himself. That kind of reward is short-lived and in the end is wholly unfulfilling.

"Austin, the only way you will ever truly be great is when you realize that all you do is in the service of the king. The glory you seek must never be for you, but for him; the battles you win must never be for you, but for him. For the man who seeks his own glory finds only his own demise. These are not easy words, Austin, but truer words you will never find. This is the third important thing you must remember."

"Master," inquired Austin as he pondered the words of Sapientius, "when you began teaching me, you said there were four things I must remember. You have told me only three. What is the fourth?"

"I have not told you the fourth because you already have it, deep within you. One of your most admirable attributes is your intensity and fervor. You love what you do and it affects those around you. Therefore, the fourth thing is that you must continue to be passionate in your service. I charge you always to remain energetic, vibrant, and hopeful. May each new day be a pleasant surprise in the service of your king."

Austin obeyed the words of his master. And in all the kingdom, the name of Austin the Great has been legendary throughout the ages.

THE FOUR P'S

There were four things Austin needed to achieve the greatness he sought:

1. To know himself, his talents, and his abilities would be essential for discovering his *Purpose*.
2. To know the value of camaraderie and love, he needed to have *People* in his life.
3. To do all his work in the service of the king required *Praise*.
4. And finally, to function with intensity and fervor would call for *Passion*.

The story of Austin the Great describes the fruits of my quest for the few right things that matter. They are Passion, Purpose, People, and Praise — simple, powerful, necessary, and all-inclusive areas for reinventing the life you want.

When all is said and done, the easiest way is usually the hardest way.

As I said, my search for the Four Ps involved reading, interviewing, and observing. But in all my research, one resource influenced my conclusions more than any other. In fact, this resource provided me with the whole foundation for the Four Ps. That resource was the Bible, which shouldn't be surprising when you consider that an obvious source for finding the meaning of life is the Creator of life.

In a very familiar section in the Gospel of Matthew, Jesus is approached by a group of religious leaders, one of whom asks him, "Teacher, what is the most important commandment of the Law?" Jesus tells them it's simple: "The greatest commandment is to 'Love the Lord your God with all your heart, all your soul, and all your mind.' The second is like the first, 'Love your neighbor as yourself.'"

In two simple sentences, Jesus describes a few things that really matter to God. First is a focus on an inner relationship with God — praise. Second is a focus on loving God's highest creation — people.

When Jesus says to love your neighbor "as yourself," he shows that the prerequisite to loving others effectively is a healthy love or respect of self. And I believe we love and respect ourselves most when we live according to our God-given purpose. Hence the third P is "purpose."

The fourth is passion. Jesus calls for total commitment — heart, soul, and mind. Passion serves as the driving force for all the other Ps, fueling our quest for a life that matters.

Passion, purpose, people, and praise. Besides their simplicity, one of the beauties of the Four Ps is the honor they give to each individual. They're not about telling you what you should or shouldn't do. They're not even about telling you how to behave. They're about helping you consider what's important in life — to you, to those you love, and to God.

Let's look at the Four Ps in slightly more detail.

Passion

When I was in seminary, I discovered a fascinating word used only a few times in the Greek New Testament — *splanknon*. Although it is generally translated as "affection" or "heart," it carries a slightly different meaning than you might imagine. For instance, in his letter to the Philippians, Paul says, "how I long for you with the *affection* of Christ" (NASB) and in 1 John we read about a person "closing his *heart*" to someone in need (NASB). In both cases, "affection" and "heart" translate the Greek word *splanknon*.

Splanknon is rich with depth and feeling. In fact, the Greek dictionary describes *splanknon* as the source of significant human action, the "seat of passion." I love the idea of having a place within each of us that is the *seat of passion* — a wonderful and healthy drive to love, live, serve, and succeed. People who make an impact and live a life that matters are seriously passionate about what they do. They have a contagious zeal for life. But their passion isn't automatic. It takes work. They nurture and develop their "seat of passion," and they know that without it, meaning and purpose in life are almost impossible to find.

Several years ago, a friend of mine was waiting to get his hair cut when he overheard one guy giving advice to another. "This ain't no dress rehearsal," he said. "You won't get to do this thing a second time." The line has stuck with me because it is so true. You only get one life, and you would like to give this one your best shot. And your very best shot would certainly include a passionate pursuit of a life of impact.

Purpose

Another of the few things that will really matter is for you to create a vision of your present and your future life. It will require spending serious time asking yourself, "Who do I really want to be?" In order to offer any meaning at all, this vision or dream must be based on a genuine understanding of your own talents, skills, and desires. When you give yourself the freedom and permission to be true to those important ideas, then you are fulfilling your true purpose.

But so many external influences confuse the pursuit of a genuine self-understanding. Some people — parents, bosses, coworkers, pastors, friends — may want to recreate you in their own image. They have preconceived ideas of who you should be, what you should do, and how you should love. What's more, you may allow yourself to be recreated in the image of someone else. The result is that you're frustrated and unfulfilled.

The truth is, you were already created in someone else's image, the image of God. And your task is to devote your life to making choices that authenticate your God-given self. A life of fulfilled purpose is one where you make significant contributions and achieve rewarding accomplishments based on who you are.

People

An American catastrophe that is growing to frightening proportions is the tragic number of crimes conducted by children and youth. Only this morning I read in the Opinion section of the *LA Times* that at our current pace we are approaching an almost ungovernable situation. Kids with hollow stares and virtually no values commit murder for a mere twenty bucks. Police, prison, and punishment bring absolutely no fear to their hearts. Why?

The kids I read about are unparented and unloved. Raised by mothers on crack and abandoned by dads, they've never known the kind of love that doesn't give up on them, a love that disciplines with the goal of developing character, one that loves them for no good reason. Having never known this kind of love, they hold little or no value for dignity and human life.

The human animal dies (and kills) when it knows not love. The human need for other people is first for survival, then for satisfaction, and finally for significance. The "people" factor in the equation is vital for all of us, not just kids in trouble. For that reason, a person seeking a life of impact and purpose will always be diligent about his or her relationships. People are certainly not "things," but they are always the right "things" to take precedence in our lives.

Praise

The fourth of the "few things that matter" is the one that matters most. Saint Augustine and Blaise Pascal both said it: "There is a vacuum in the soul of every person that can be filled by no created thing, but by the Creator alone." It is the most basic human need — the need to know and worship God.

Worship of God is not something you choose to do; it is something you are driven to do because it is a part of your nature. In vain attempts to fill that God-shaped hole, some people focus on personal success (overemphasis on Purpose) and others focus on a person or people (overemphasis on People). But a few people find God and in doing so discover a rich life of gratitude and praise.

The few things that matter — Passion, Purpose, People, and Praise. There is nothing revolutionary here. In fact, they're rather obvious. But because of all our other distractions, they're easy to forget. Yet they are essential.

The Four Ps are the foundation for *getting the right things right* because they are the right things. Everything you do in life will fall into one of these domains. Therefore, every chapter will directly relate to one or more of them as they are interwoven throughout.

The Four Ps don't suggest specific things for you to do. Instead, they offer what strategic planners call "high level direction." They look at your life from the forty-thousand-foot level, focusing on the long term. The application of these principles is quite different from what you'll find in an ordinary planning tool. Applying these principles is not about prioritization, nor is it about balance. It's actually about the opposite.

PRIORITIES, BALANCE, AND UNREASONABLE THINKING

Consider another "unreasonable thought." Occasions arise when it is not only OK but advisable that you live intentionally out of balance.

First, take the concept of high-level priorities. You're familiar with them. They're the ones that suggest putting God first, family second, and work third. While those priorities look nice on paper, they don't do real well in the real world. Sometimes they don't even make sense.

Think about it. What does it mean to place God first? The concept has little meaning when you consider that God is involved in everything you do, like it or not. God doesn't come first. He comes first, second, third, fourth, and fiftieth. Life with God cannot be so compartmentalized.

Then what does it mean to put family second? Does it mean that any and all of your family's needs supersede your career or your friends' needs? In the 1995 NFL playoffs the backup quarterback for one of the teams announced that he wouldn't show up for the first-round playoff game if his pregnant wife went into labor that day. He stated his rationale as the priorities of God first, family second, and work third.

I make no judgments on this man's decision. I support the right of every man and woman to determine their own ethical choices. I even admire his brave decision to buck the system and go with the integrity of his beliefs and conscience. The world could use more people adhering to their principles.

But I do question the rationale for his decision. Does it really work? In order to live up to his priority of family over work, he had to break his word. He is under contract to suit up for games — especially playoff games. To maintain his priority, he had to break his word to the owners, his teammates, and the people of a large city. The Bible goes so far as to suggest that giving your word to a man is part and parcel with giving your word to God. If that is indeed true, it appears this man broke his first priority to God in order to honor the second priority to his family.

Does commitment to family mean that anytime your husband or wife makes a request you are duty bound to respond, no matter what the sacrifice to your career? Of course not. Sometimes you must place the long-term needs of your career over the immediate needs of your family. It may be a very difficult decision, but it can also be the most appropriate one. More on this later.

Another common life-planning concept I struggle with is the principle of balance — the idea that you need to live a "balanced life" in which you devote equal time to certain high-level priorities. Like the previous illustration, this philosophy suggests you must strike a balance between God and family and work and friends. If at any time you get "out of balance" and spend too much time in one area, you may be headed for disaster.

I believe just the opposite. I believe at times the demands of life require that you intentionally live out of balance.

Rather than balance or prioritization, the Four Ps system suggests integration. At any given point in life you may not be "in balance," but you can integrate each of the few things that matter.

Let's say, for example, that you have just landed a management position with a start-up company. For the next year, you will be expected to work a minimum of fifty-five to sixty hours per week, often even more. In the Passion, Purpose, People, Praise matrix it appears that you will be spending all of your time in the Purpose area — quite out of balance.

Life by nature is out of balance; the trick is to have an act.

Instead, consider how you can *integrate* all of the key areas in the midst of your temporary and necessary out-of-balance state. Integration might take this form: You maintain *passion* because you're doing something you love, and you also eke out a little time for a movie or a play. Your *purpose* is being highly fulfilled because of your high level of accomplishment. *People* can be integrated because you are working on a team and also because you regularly consult with your spouse about business issues, and you devote limited, but regular time to friends. *Praise* is the easiest one to integrate because you know that start-ups have an inordinately high failure rate, so you regularly pray about your work.

At certain times in life it's advisable to have a more singular focus — in times of crisis, of personal improvement, of need (e.g. job requirements), of stress or depression, or when you fall in love. Being out of balance can be great. Just remember that it is normally only a temporary state, and it still requires some integration of the Four Ps.

Again, the beauty of the Four Ps system is the way in which it honors you. It honors your reason, your relationships, and your spirituality. The system allows you to make hard choices by using wisdom instead of a overly simplistic template. And the key to the Four Ps is that it does not imply aiming at one high-level target (like a certain career) as much as it does integrating the critical values and activities it takes to get there.

In your own process of reinventing yourself, there are at least four things you'll want to get right. Be *passionate* about what you do; understand and pursue your God-given *purpose*; love, serve, and depend on the *people* around you; and intentionally give your attention and *praise* to God. Integrate them in all you do as you reinvent the life you want.

Right Turns

RECALL THE RIGHT IDEAS

- Each of us has a "Mary" and a "Martha." We need both, but our "Mary" side is usually the most neglected.
- We are bombarded by dozens of choices and "important" matters to attend to every day. But really, only a few things are necessary.
- The few right things that really matter fall into four categories, the Four Ps: Passion, Purpose, People, and Praise.
- Life rarely cooperates with a plan for balance. The best plan

may feel out of balance at times, but it adjusts for and integrates key areas.

DECIDE WHAT'S RIGHT FOR YOU

- In what way does your life feel out of balance right now?
- How do you normally respond or cope when your life feels this way?
- What activities would you list from your life under each of the Four Ps?
- Which of the four areas do you hope to change most as you reinvent the life you want?

MAKE THE RIGHT MOVES

- Think of one right thing in each of the P categories that you want to do this week.
- Give yourself permission to be temporarily out of balance.
- But, create a timeline for when you will get back to a more fully integrated lifestyle.
- Write "Mary" and "Martha" at the top of a page. List your own personality traits under the appropriate columns. Do you identify more with Mary or Martha? How might you build up the other side?

When the artist is alive in any person, whatever his kind of work may be, he becomes an inventive, searching, daring, self-expressive creature. He becomes interesting to other people; he disturbs, upsets, and opens ways for better understanding.
Where those who are not artists are trying to close the book, he opens it and shows there are still more pages.

ROBERT HENRI

Whatever your hand finds to do, verily, do it with all your might....

ECCLESIASTES 9:10, NASB

CHAPTER THREE

REAWAKENINGS

W hen you think of "passion," what comes to mind? For most of us, the first thing is the heat of romance. Books by Danielle Steele. Movies with Sharon Stone and Michael Douglas. It's unfortunate, but true; in the last twenty years we have come to confuse passion with sex. But true, deep-seated, unrelenting passion is far more than a sex act. It is about the very drive for existence, the love of life, and the ultimate regard for the wonder of all creation.

Passion is the steam that fuels our reinventive engines. Without a passionate drive and a passionate heart, I fear we would have little motivation to pursue the life we want. Therefore the final thing we need to *think right* before we *act right* concerns the way we approach the whole process of reinventing ourselves — our passionate approach.

AWAKE PEOPLE

Don't laugh, but *Joe vs. the Volcano* with Tom Hanks and Meg Ryan is one of my all-time favorite movies. I know it's weird, it's silly, it's slow, but it's also very provocative. It shows a slice of life that many of us are too familiar with, the slice of life that is boring, repetitious, and mundane. As well, the movie offers hope.

In one of its great scenes Meg Ryan and Tom Hanks are discussing the life-threatening dangers of an adventure Hanks is about to undertake. He has agreed to sail a long distance to a small island inhabited by villagers who expect him to jump into a volcano — an act of appeasement to the volcano to prevent it from erupting. In this conversation Hanks appears ready to back out. But before he has a chance to quit, Ryan says to him, "You know, my daddy says, 'Almost the whole world is asleep. Only a handful of people are awake, and they live in a state of constant amazement.'"

Those words struck me like a spear. Awake people living in a state of constant amazement. Of course! We need more awake people! Awake people who are passionate about living and experiencing life on this planet of wonder — a planet created by an act of wonder. We need awake people to stimulate us and to draw us out of dreariness. It's far too easy to fall asleep and drudge around as if drugged by the everydayness of it all, catatonic from boredom, fear, loss, or rejection.

How many truly awake people do you know? They're easy to spot. They are interesting and sometimes energetic. They are the kind of people you just like to be around. They seem to sense the awesomeness of life, and they have a tendency to make it contagious. Don't get me wrong; passionate people do not live in "la la land." They are not hopeless romantics who thrive on denial and simply pretend the world is a rosy place. Just the opposite. They are stark realists who know there is a dark side, generally because they have had more experience with the dark side of life than they would like to tell you. But they don't let dark reality overwhelm the possibility of a bright future. They may be disappointed, but not disheartened; frazzled, but not fried.

I think we all desire passion. We look enviously at those people who have that *joie de vivre* and wonder "What makes them so dog-gone lucky?" Maybe we just need to be reawakened, as if from a long slumber. Maybe we can be passionate too. And maybe, just maybe, passion has more to do with choice than with luck.

Just because your eyes are open doesn't mean you're awake.

I have found passionately awake people to be both deeply feeling and deeply caring. They have experienced enough of life's difficulties to relate to the struggles and joys of others. When I think of passionate people, I think of Abraham Lincoln, Thomas Jefferson, Martin Luther King Jr., Mohammed Ali, Maya Angelou, Millard Williams, Frederick Buechner, Mary Graves, and Denny Bellesi. Some of these people you have heard of, some not. Some are famous as politicians, writers, athletes. Others are just regular people like you and me. But all of them are truly distinct.

THE PASSIONATE DISTINCTIVE

Denny Bellesi is just a regular guy. He's a five-foot-ten, one-hundred-sixty-five-pound Italian who loves people, pasta, and golf. Everybody likes Denny; everybody trusts Denny — for a reason. While Denny Bellesi is just a regular guy, he's no ordinary guy, not by a long shot. Some people call him crazy, some call him a visionary. I call him passionate.

Denny Bellesi was the youth pastor of a large church in North Los Angeles County. One day he took a drive south, as far as South Orange County, almost a hundred miles. He took an exit off the freeway, found a place to park, and stopped his car. As he sat there, he became convinced this was the place he should start a church. He had no contacts, no friends in the area, no building permits. He had nothing except his belief.

So Denny quit his job, moved to Orange County, and found a dozen people as nutty as himself, and they started midweek gatherings as the genesis for their new church. As you have probably guessed, the gatherings grew and grew and grew. Now, ten years later, Denny Bellesi is the senior pastor of Coast Hills Community Church with two dozen full-time staff and a weekly attendance of more than fifteen hundred people.

Those who called him crazy were probably right to some degree. Those who called him a visionary were definitely right. But I still contend it was Denny's passion that was his greatest asset. He believed in what he was doing. He believed in God. He believed in people. And his passionate beliefs were so contagious that he is now surrounded by folks with the same passion, passing it on to others.

I've made a habit of observing passionate people to identify what sets them apart. What qualities does someone like Denny have that the rest of us can incorporate into our lives? Can passion be learned? To some degree, you bet, because passionate people are characterized by being hopeful, seeing life as an adventure, being true "believers," being grateful.

They Are Hopeful

The movie *Shawshank Redemption* is based on the true story of one man who refused to abandon hope while spending twenty years of his life in prison. Several times in the movie I was reminded that we need no bars or walls or cells to be in prison. We create our own. Think of your prison walls. Are they made of financial security? Or other people's approval? Or personal insecurity? When we submit to these perceived limitations, we fail to embrace life as an adventure.

The *Shawshank Redemption* illustrated for me that we have much more control over our destiny than I had ever considered. If a man in prison could refuse to allow his soul to be eaten up by that horrid institution, and if he could retain hope while spending twenty years there, what stops us from doing the same thing when we are free?

A few years ago I was part of a "covenant group" — a group of twelve guys who got together one time each year for three or four days. The mission of our group was to create a safe and confidential environment where each guy could "unpack" personal issues that had arisen over the past year. We were also committed to cutthroat volleyball competition and serious fun.

In one of our sessions we got into a discussion about the relationship of hope and melancholia. The question was posed, "Which do you believe: Clouds will always follow a sunny day, or the sun always shines after a storm?" It's an important question. An asleep person will tend to say, "Clouds always follow the sun. Don't get too happy about it being good today because tomorrow will always bring more sorrow." But the person of passion, the reawakened person, sees clouds as a natural, but only temporary, part of life. They believe "the sun also rises."

In other words, they are people of hope. They have hope for themselves and hope for the people around them. A friend of mine once said the Christian distinctive is hope. That is what sets Christianity apart from all other religions.

In Christianity there is always hope for change — from old and destructive ways to new and better ways.

There is hope for forgiveness — nothing is done that can't be forgiven.

There is hope for life — present and eternal.

There is hope for relationship — an intimate relationship with other people and with God.

They See Life As an Adventure

Because passionate people are so hopeful, they approach life as if it were an adventure. In the past twenty-five years, I've had four distinct careers. Over time, I've learned to approach life adventurously. I am now crazy enough to believe that if one career doesn't work out, I can always find another. But it wasn't always so.

My first career was in carpet manufacturing, where I ended up as manager of the wet-processing department. I stayed in that career for twelve years, in one company for ten. In fact, it was on my tenth anniversary that I quit. Unfortunately I wasn't there ten years because I loved it — I hated it for at least five years. But I was stuck. I was comfortable. I was afraid of change. I was asleep!

Then, at thirty-two years old I quit, went to seminary for three years (yes, it only took three years), and became a pastor. After six years in the ministry, I started another career and became a management consultant, working primarily with petroleum engineering firms like Chevron and Aramco. And today, I have launched a new company, one that is committed to the personal and spiritual development of people like you and me.

Some sleep while they live; others live what they dream.

Life has become an adventure. While I regularly face difficulties, setbacks, and personal discouragement, somewhere deep inside is this kid who looks at life as if it were one giant playground filled with new and fun things to try.

It doesn't take a radical career change or other dramatic circumstances for you to see life as an adventure. The act of loving is adventurous. Daily, each new opportunity and each new challenge create adventure. Seeing life as an adventure depends on conscious choice, not circumstances.

They Are "Believers"

A third quality I've noticed in the passionate is that they believe in something. They frequently have a cause and are strongly committed to it. It may be an organizational cause, like the environment, cancer research, or politics. It may be a personal cause like faith, integrity, or decency. It can even be gardening. It doesn't have to be a cause that anybody else buys into because what others think is of little importance to the passionately focused person. Whatever the cause or belief, a passionate person will not be wishy-washy.

There was a time when the USA was filled with women and men dedicated to their beliefs. We were once proud to take a stand. But I fear we may be losing our edge. We're getting soft. Have you noticed how "middle of the road" we have become? So many positions and so many issues create even more confusion and dispel clarity. That may be why the most popular political position today is *moderate*. Moderate can be a great position when it is the deliberate result of wrestling with the issues. But it is a terribly sad position when it serves more as an excuse for not thinking.

By contrast, Denny Bellesi is a "believer." When he started Coast Hills, he believed in himself, in his cause, in the people with him, and in the support of his God. These beliefs became the focus for his passion, a foundation not easily rocked.

Passionate people believe! And their belief creates energy for their cause, which even further fuels their passion.

They Are Grateful

Show me a passionate person, and I'll show you someone who is thankful for all he has. Grateful people look at "good things" as gifts. They know deep within themselves they don't really deserve to be as fortunate as they are.

The passionate people I know *expect* little from life, and they don't feel they are *owed* anything. Their perspective is counter to our cultural concept of "rights." In the last twenty-five years we have radically distorted what the founding fathers had in mind when they said that all people are "born with certain inalienable rights." Somehow this has come to mean that every person has the right to own and experience equal blessings. Not only is this not true, it is damaging.

If I believe it is "my right" to have a good marriage or to have a son or to have a certain kind of job, then I come to expect those things. If "it's my right" to have them, then the likelihood of my being grateful for those things is small. In a very real sense, I am robbed of one of the most passionate emotions available to me, the wonderful emotion of gratitude.

Do you know one of life's greatest ways of making us grateful? Overcoming adversity. Grateful people often had a difficult childhood, suffered troubling losses, or had to compete against the odds. And they succeeded. But in doing so, they realized they could just as easily have failed. Although they worked hard, they know that "success" was a gift.

In 1995 I facilitated a team session with public-affairs executives from a large, multinational organization, which included the corporate vice president and his direct reports. At one point we were asked about the kind of home we were raised in. To my surprise, each of the nine participants — all very high level — came from rather humble, modest homes. In fact, I don't recall that any of the parents had a college education. Instead, they had strong values and strong work ethics. These executives had nothing handed to them on a platter. They worked hard to get where they were. And with a lot of talent, a lot of hard work, and a bit of luck, they were among the most successful in one of the world's most respected corporations. And one more interesting thing about these folks — they emanated gratitude for their jobs and for their families. These were indeed passionate people.

THE DIFFICULTY WITH PASSION

Sometimes it's difficult to be an awake person. So many daily trials rob us of our passion. In *Joe vs. the Volcano*, Tom Hanks was afraid of being totally out of control. Until he could overcome that fear, he was robbed of his passion. He truly had to take a "leap of faith," (and those of you who saw the movie know it was a "literal" leap of faith).

Each day brings a new problem, another difficulty for us to deal with. We suffer loss (family, friends, possessions, careers); we experience rejection; and we fail, over and over and over again. All of these difficulties are "numb-ers." They're like an anesthetic. In order not to feel the hurt again, we simply elect not to feel at all. And we fall asleep, going through each day numb, all passion gone. I have seen too many visionaries fail here.

At some undetectable point, the proverbial straw lands on the camel's back, and we just give in. We give up by giving in to our circumstances. We succumb to the powers that be, whoever it is "up there," or to those who seem to have it in for us.

Making magical music is more than merely reducing your mistakes.

Although life does have a way of dealing out difficulties, passionate people accept them as simply a normal part of life. Scott Peck nailed it on the head in *The Road Less Traveled* when he wrote, "Life is difficult.... Once we fully embrace the truth that life is difficult — when we truly understand and accept it — then life is no longer difficult. Because once it is accepted, the fact that life is difficult no longer matters." When we truly grasp that fact, we are ready to pursue renewed passion for life.

THE PASSION OF GOD

No, being passionate about life is not always easy. There will be times when you just don't feel like it; times when you feel alone and discouraged; times when you barely have your head above water, when you're up to your armpits in alligators. What do you do then? Is it possible to create passion? Can you just invent it and then drop it into your soul?

No, you can't create passion. But the good news is you don't have to because it has already been created for you. The propensity for passion lies within you, just waiting for you to draw it out. It originates in the very depths of your soul, placed there from the beginning of time by the Creator. Passion is part of what theologians call the *imago dei*, the image of God in which you and I were created. You were created in the likeness of a very passionate God. Scripture contains scores of examples.

The first example of God's passion is in Genesis chapter one where God completes his creative work of art in six stages. At the end of each stage he exclaims, "It is good!" This is no small statement when you consider that "good" is a relative term; it must be compared to something in order to have meaning. In this situation the only thing around to compare to is God himself — perfection. So what sounds like a mere statement, "It is good," might be better rendered, "Wow, look at what I've done! This is perfect!" A statement of great passion.

Since the birth of my son I have a much better grasp on what might have been in the heart of the Creator when he said, "It is good." Pam and I were married when I was thirty-five and she was thirty-two. We both wanted a family but felt we could wait a while. After three years of marriage we finally decided to have a baby. But we didn't anticipate that getting pregnant wouldn't be so simple for a thirty-eight-year-old man and a thirty-five-year-old woman.

Four years, two miscarriages, and scores of doctors' appointments later, Austin was born. It was good. Boy, was it good! As much as I loved my wife, I had no idea I had that much love inside of me. At the birth of Austin, Pam and I experienced passion enough for a lifetime.

Pam and I had created life, a life that was the full reflection of the two of us. And I believe that is the same passion God must have felt after his creation, the master stroke of the creation of all that is. It is the same passion of God that is available to all of us.

In Genesis chapter nine, after releasing a flood that destroyed mankind, God in his mercy said he would never do such a thing again. Instead, he chose to be "long-suffering," that is to "suffer long" for his creation. His passion for his creation was so great that he chose personal suffering over the annihilation of the earth. In the same way, we see how Jesus chose to suffer on the cross for the good of his creation. Historically we have called this act "The Passion of Christ."

It takes many mistakes to make a great life.

We ought to pursue our lives with that same intensity of passion. If we were to consciously link our passion with that of God, perhaps we would focus more on doing the right things than on doing things right.

In his book on grace entitled *Between Noon and Three*, Robert Farrar Capon speaks of the tendency of the religious to misplace their focus. Religiosity, he contends, emphasizes the rules when it would be better to emphasize the reasons behind the rules and go to the core of "true religion" where we find giving and loving relationships. He says the church for too long has focused on rules over relationship, and as a result we have become like "ill taught piano students," more concerned with making flubs than making music.

Too true. The concern for making flubs is one of the quickest ways I know to destroy personal passion. If you don't believe me, ask any five-year-old to sing a song, and listen to that child belt it out. Ask an adult to do the same thing, and the likely response will be something like, "Oh, I can't sing." I say yes, you can.

The process of reinventing yourself can be an incredibly passionate one. Let's forget our concern for making flubs. Let's forget that life is difficult. So what? Instead, let's be the ones who make symphonic music so explosive and inviting that it awakens all the dreary sleepers surrounding us. May we be as musical lights to the world, bringing delight wherever we go as we reflect the creative passion of the Creator of the universe.

Right Turns

RECALL THE RIGHT IDEAS

- Without passion, it is an effort to find the energy and inspiration required to reinvent one's life.
- Many people are not truly awake to their lives. They have

fallen asleep and have forgotten how to experience passion.

- We have passion inherently because we were made out of God's passion. It can't be manufactured, but it can be called forth.
- Passionate people are grateful, adventurous, and filled with wonder.

DECIDE WHAT'S RIGHT FOR YOU

- What do you love to do? When was the last time you did it?
- What about life fills you with wonder? Can you list five things quickly?
- Describe the last time you had an "adventure."
- What is the difference between emotions, feelings, and passions?

MAKE THE RIGHT MOVES

- This week do one thing you really love to do.
- Dig up (or think up) some old art or writing attempts from childhood. Who were you then? What mysterious things were you longing to say?
- Make a list of things you are grateful for. Do you "deserve" any of them?
- Spend a half-hour staring at a small bug in the lawn, a leaf's veins, or a baby sleeping.

PART TWO

Recovering Your Inner Assets

What are you worth?

After getting your thinking right, it's time to do some investigation. All business endeavors begin with a research/data gathering phase. What data do you need to initiate a personal reinvention?

Any viable effort to reinvent the life you really want begins with a solid understanding of who you are by creation. From there you can more clearly envision the "you" that you want to be — your dream.

One of our problems is that very few of us have developed any distinctive personal life. Everything about us seems secondhand.

ALAN JONES
FROM JOURNEY INTO CHRIST

"For God sees not as man sees, for man looks at the outward appearance, but the LORD looks at the heart."

1 SAMUEL 16:7, NASB

CHAPTER FOUR

WRONG RULES

D ennis and Joni lived in the apartment next door when I was a sophomore at UCLA. Because they had already reached the ripe old age of twenty-nine, my roommate and I called them Mom and Dad, which gives you an idea how young we were.

I knew them for only one year, but my memories are vivid. Dennis loved to sail, and he was what you might call a purist. We used to crew for him when he'd race his 27' Thunderbird, an older, solid-wood boat. The Thunderbird class is generally much slower than the newer, fiberglass boats, but something about purists makes them love old things, especially when these old things are made of wood.

Dennis was also a professor of botany at UCLA, which is no small accomplishment for a twenty-nine-year-old. Toward the end of our year as neighbors, Dennis got the offer of a lifetime — a research and teaching position at a university in Puerto Rico, one of the sailing capitals of the world. I remember his excitement. "I get to do research, I get to teach, and I get to sail. What a dream come true!"

Two years later I received interesting news about Dennis. He had quit his teaching position and moved to Galveston, Texas, to become a boat builder. His move shocked many colleagues and friends. Dennis tossed aside his highly respected position as a university professor for a totally different kind of work, a kind that wouldn't necessarily command the respect he had become used to. His Ph.D. would impress no one in the boatyard. But it was a career move that tapped into the seat of passion in Dennis' heart, a place that botany failed to touch.

Dennis devoted more than a decade of his life to getting his Ph.D., investing thousands of hours of study. But in the end he discovered that he had climbed the wrong ladder of success. There came a point when Dennis finally admitted to himself, "This isn't me. I'm not a botanist. I'm not a researcher. And I'm not a teacher. I am a boat builder."

WRONG RULES

Dennis' story is not unique. My wife, Pam, is a seasoned career counselor, having spent fourteen years in this booming field. Every day she encounters people at all levels of business and in all types of work who are extremely frustrated with their careers. A surprising number of these dissatisfied people are professionals, often with several degrees, who have attained enviable success in their business but have experienced little personal satisfaction. It is increasingly apparent that we have a cultural epidemic of dissatisfaction with work.

The real issue, however, is not jobs and careers. Dissatisfaction with work merely reflects a generic failure to experience any true sense of accomplishment in life. Remember the Four Ps: passion, purpose, people, and praise? The "purpose" piece is missing from the puzzle of their lives, and it's the piece that's often the most perplexing. One factor that makes it so is our poor understanding of "who we are built to be" in the first place.

What you have now is often worth more than what you want.

In his writings on life and work, modern-day contemplative Basil Pennington declares, "It is your life's work to learn to think and act in accord with who you are by creation." At first glance this would not seem so difficult a task, yet it is the rare individual who both has a good understanding of self and also does something about it.

A primary reason we fail "to think and act in accord with who we are by creation" is quite simply "wrong rules." From our earliest years we are taught to please, to admire, and to mimic other people. In doing so, we neglect to look inside ourselves to find out who God has wonderfully created.

A few months ago I read an article about tennis great Andre Agassi. For many years Agassi lived according to the adage "Image is everything," which says it doesn't really matter who you are inside, it's what you look like that counts. Then in 1994–95 something changed Agassi. He became more in tune with himself. He describes his transition as going from "painfully self-conscious" to "gratefully self-aware." If you follow tennis, you know that Agassi is now playing his best tennis ever.

THE PIT OF SELF-CONSCIOUSNESS

For Agassi — and for you and me — the pit of self-consciousness is a dismal hole that refuses to be filled. The descent into this viscous pit begins by placing such an overemphasis on other people that you lose awareness of your own natural distinctiveness. This overemphasis on other people will cause you to be "out of focus" and, in the long run, will hinder significant living. Let's consider three ways you might get offtrack:

- When you focus on other people's desires;
- When you focus on other people's accomplishments;
- When you focus on other people's needs.

A Focus on Others' Desires

I was raised with the saying "You can be anybody you want to be and do anything you want to do if you only put your mind to it." It's a great idea, one that has motivated millions of people. There's only one problem: It's not wholly true. There is truth in it — you can accomplish far

72

more than you think if you work hard enough and smart enough. But you cannot do or be *anything*. You are limited by who you are.

For instance, I could never be a concert pianist or a professional basketball player or a surgeon or a dentist. I don't have the physical talents to perform those highly skilled tasks. Neither could I be a therapist who specializes in long-term care or a corporate human-resources specialist. I don't have the talents or patience to work with slow and minimal change. I'm "built" to do other things, and when I'm doing those things, I receive much more satisfaction from my efforts.

Many people visit career counseling offices because they attained success in fields that are outside their natural talents. They learned to excel, but not enjoy. And many times these pursuits originated from people who had great influence on their lives.

Our son, Austin, is three years old. He's very cool. Already we make observations and speculate on his talents. Like his mom, he is gregarious; we call it "socially bold." One afternoon at daycare a mom who was visiting the school brought her son into the large playroom. Austin immediately went up to the boy and attempted to welcome this fellow three-year-old. When the new boy responded shyly and didn't say anything, Austin looked at the mom and questioned with genuine concern, "Does he talk?"

He also seems to have my proclivity for reasoning. He thinks logically. When he asks "why?" it's because he really wants to understand. We've observed his leadership skills at daycare. And we are told that he is unusually caring. If a friend is crying, he will put his arm around the child and say, "That's okay. Don't cry."

When he grows up, he might make a fine career counselor like his mom, or even a writer or consultant like me. Wouldn't that be great?

You see how easy it is? If I continue to think along the lines I just described, I may manage to direct my son's future with far more specificity than he'll ever need. I run the risk of squelching the child God has created. My job as a parent is to teach my son love, obedience, morality, and the awesomeness of God; to help him know when to be kind and when to be firm; to encourage his talents and to stretch him in his weaknesses; and to overwhelm him with love and loving discipline.

My job as a parent is *not* to direct my son to a certain career. And yet that is what too many parents do. Do you know why? Because many of us were raised that way. In her career counseling, my wife says that one of the most destructive messages her clients must deal with is the parental message. "You should be a doctor...a lawyer...a painter...a teacher...or, heaven forbid, a writer." And even when that parental message is rejected, it sticks.

So the question is "Whose message do you hear?" Is it a parent's? How about one from a favorite teacher? Or from a group of friends? Or from your pastor? I couldn't count the number of men in my seminary who entered the ministry because they were encouraged by their pastor or their parents, but they had never really evaluated the full scope of pastoral requirements in light of their own talents, skills, and desires. As a result, we see a tragically high number of pastors and ministers dropping out of the ministry, or worse, wanting to drop out but having no idea where to turn.

The influential desires of parents, teachers, bosses, and pastors have probably proven quite helpful in guiding your actions. But until they are melded with the desires of your own heart, they will wane in effectiveness and may eventually get in the way of personally meaningful accomplishments.

A Focus on Others' Accomplishments

Mentors, role models, and idols. All very helpful. All potentially destructive.

Mentors and role models provide two helpful services. One is to portray for you an ideal or a goal, and the other is to offer hope that you, too, might be able to accomplish it. We find an excellent illustration of "biblical role modeling" in the New Testament when Paul suggested that the people in the church at Philippi should "join with others in following my example…and take note of those who live according to the pattern we gave you."

Although role modeling is vital for human development, it becomes problematic when we focus on a role model's (or anyone else's) *accomplishments* rather than his *character* and *manner*. Take Michael Jordan, perhaps the greatest basketball player ever to walk onto a court. Many kids idolize Michael Jordan and see him as a role model.

But, because he is so inordinately successful, a hero like Michael Jordan can be a mixed model. If kids follow his example on the court — his moves, his instincts, his drive, his compassion for his team-mates, and his respect for opposing players — they could do extremely well on and off the court. But if they attempt to be as wealthy as Michael Jordan, or as powerful as Michael Jordan, or as influential as Michael Jordan, they will miss the point that wealth, power, and influence are merely the results of hard work and character. The problem is placing the focus on what someone else has accomplished.

But there is a second and even more pervasive problem — placing too much focus on "what someone else has." And it relates to everyone you know — your next-door neighbor, your colleagues at work, people at church, your family and friends. Every day we are barraged with the temptation to focus on the possessions of other people, and along with it is an acute likelihood of losing touch with our own values and gifts. We gradually slip into those ever-consuming sins of greed, jealousy, and covetousness — those sins that swallow us up like Jonah's whale. We become driven to acquire, which keeps our eyes eternally focused away from ourselves and away from the values we were created to follow.

I live in Orange County, California, often called the "Yuppie Capital of the World." Materialism is a god here. Sometime ago I read a statistic which claimed there were more Mercedes Benzes sold in Orange County than in the rest of the country combined. Image is very important here. And no matter how much I try to reject the influence of materialism, it's almost impossible not to get caught up in it. Everybody else always has something I want — new cars, surround sound 35" televisions with movies on compact disc, leather jackets, clothes by Giorgio Armani and Jhane Barnes, right houses in the right neighborhoods, cellular phones. Of course, they shop in the right stores and eat in the right restaurants, as well.

If I am not deliberate in my quest for significance, these *things* will certainly provide a barrier. My focus switches from intrinsic to extrinsic values, to acquisitions. But no matter how many "toys" I have, I'm still the same guy.

Emulating the life of people we admire gives a tangible and reliable model to follow. Human beings were created to follow; even leaders are followers. But the key questions are these: How do you use the data? How do you estimate the worth and practicality in your own life? Do this other person's successes really fit you? If so, use them. If not, forget them, no matter how tempting.

A Focus on Others' Needs

I had been involved in the Christian faith for only a couple of years when I informed the senior pastor of our church that I was considering leaving the area to help start a new church in a location with a growing population. His first question was simple: "Why?"

My response was equally simple. "Because there is a need."

His next comment startled me. "Never do anything based solely on need," he said.

I was flabbergasted. I thought that's what the church was all about, meeting the needs of people in communities around the world. He then explained to me that the church was, indeed, about meeting needs, but that couldn't be the sole criterion for starting a church. "No matter where you go or what you do," he told me, "there will always be needs, never-ending needs."

His point was that "need" is only one of several criteria we use to determine the nature and extent of our efforts in any area. Almost fifteen years later, I still try not to do things based solely on needs. I'm much more deliberate about giving my time and finances. I ask questions — "What" am I expected to give? "How" will my gift be used? And I ask myself the very important questions — "Why" do I want to give? "Whose need" am I really trying to meet?

Never do anything based solely on need.

An alarming number of people give with an overemphasis on other people's needs — to the exclusion of nurturing and taking care of themselves. When I was a pastor, I worked with hundreds of volunteers who offered their precious free time to do the work of ministry. What a gift. Every now and then volunteers would come along who gave not just a little of their precious free time, but all of it — twenty and sometimes thirty hours a week!

I would watch these folks carefully because I didn't want them to get hurt emotionally. Some of them simply had the time to spare and loved serving. They knew their gifts and talents and how best to express them. A few others, however, were "pathological servers." They served because their "need to be needed" was greater than the needs of those they were supposed to be meeting.

So, you might ask, "What's the problem? There are needs to be met, and these people love to meet them. Who cares about the motivation? Let's leave well enough alone." My concern is *for* those people who need to be needed. It's highly unlikely they will be able to sustain any long-term effort. At some point they will break down and burn out. I have seen pastors turn to affairs and volunteers become angry at the people they are serving.

I'm not suggesting that you fail to devote your life to the service of others. I'm also not suggesting that you abandon the biblical mandate for self-sacrifice. In fact, I believe you will most fully attain significance when you serve others and make conscious choices to sacrifice yourself (more on that later). What I am saying is that before you make the choice to serve and sacrifice, consider your motivation. It's far better to sacrifice the real you, rather than the you someone else wants you to be.

BANK ACCOUNTS

A life focused on pleasing other people is a life focused on "wrong rules." It is a painfully self-conscious life which requires ceaseless evaluation about what "they" think of you, if "they" are proud, and if "they" are satisfied.

Sometimes before you can "get the right things right," you must first get rid of things you *thought* were right. Sometimes this means challenging the plans and standards friends or family have set for you. Sometimes it means bucking a cultural or societal assumption about what's right. It's okay to pursue a career that won't make you rich like your dad. It's okay to back out of a party at the last minute if you must!

As we will discuss in the next chapter, you were created with a whole host of valuable personal attributes. Think of these as assets residing in your own bank account from which you can regularly make withdrawals in order to create the life you want. When you focus on your own storehouse of attributes, you will find enough assets to last a lifetime. However, when you find yourself focusing on others' desires, accomplishments, or needs — wrong rules — you end up making withdrawals from someone else's account. These transactions will almost inevitably lead to vocational, emotional, and spiritual bankruptcy.

Because you were created with a spectacular range of talents and skills, there are multiple ways you can express them. The next chapter will help you explore your options.

Right Turns

RECALL THE RIGHT IDEAS

- From our earliest years we learn to please others. In doing so we conform ourselves to their image, rather than becoming who we were created to be.

- Before we can reinvent our lives, we must identify and throw out these "wrong rules."

- An overemphasis on other people's desires, accomplishments, and needs will ultimately lead to a pit of self-consciousness.

- We each possess a "bank account" of valuable assets we can access at any time. Why risk "bankruptcy" by trying to make withdrawals from someone else's account?

DECIDE WHAT'S RIGHT FOR YOU

- As you grew up, who had the most influence on your ideas about who you are? Was this mostly positive or negative?
- What "wrong rules" from younger days have you already discovered and tossed?
- Of the needs, accomplishments, or possessions of others, which do you focus on most?
- Have you given "wrong rules" to others? Kids? Friends? Your spouse?

MAKE THE RIGHT MOVES

- Make a list of "wrong rules" you think you subscribe to, such as "I should never say no to mother because she's very old."
- Choose only two or three "wrong rules" that you want to work on, and remember that change takes patience and focus.
- Identify future opportunities where you will respond differently when confronted with "wrong rules." For example, "Next time my sister tells me I'm not suave enough to run for public office..."
- Remember that you are ultimately responsible for the wrong rules you adopt in life, even if others introduce them.

*A time comes when you need to stop waiting for the man
you want to become and start being the man you want to be.*

BRUCE SPRINGSTEEN
FROM AN INTERVIEW ON *60 MINUTES*

It is better to be a live dog than a dead lion!

ECCLESIASTES 9:4, TLB

CHAPTER FIVE

MUST DO'S

W hen Jack Burns graduated from high school, he followed the path taken by all his friends. He went on to college. But college didn't seem to work for Jack. His interests were in other areas. Jack is a "hands man." He loves designing and building things. There wasn't enough action in college, so he quit.

After working a few jobs, Jack decided to start his own business. Since he had always loved racing boats and cars, Jack formed a company called Burns Fabrication where he designed and built customized engine parts. And to his surprise, Jack discovered he could make a living doing it. It was great — he was his own boss, set his own hours, and established his own goals, all while doing what he loved.

But there was one little problem — image. All of Jack's friends were now college graduates and had white-collar jobs. Even though, as an independent entrepreneur, Jack was doing something of equal or even greater value than his friends, he still felt that tug of insecurity from not having earned a college diploma. So Jack went back to school. Fortunately that lasted only a couple of months before he said, "Phooey, who needs a college degree anyway?" Jack finally gave himself permission to pursue his own calling, one that perfectly fit his talents, skills, interests, values, and personality.

Giving himself that permission freed up Jack to develop his business with renewed vigor. Today Burns Fabrication is an international custom engine parts company called Burns Stainless. Jack's small business now employs five people while turning over one million dollars in annual sales.

WHAT *MUST* YOU DO?

For understanding the nuts and bolts of reinventing the life you really want, this may be one of the most important chapters in the book because it's time to replace the "wrong rules" discussed in the last chapter with the "right rules," ones based on accurate self-appraisal and self-understanding. Such an exercise will affect every part of your life, even your spirituality.

Ranier Maria Rilke was a turn-of-the-century German poet. Since he was quite well known, from time to time he would receive correspondence from would-be poets. Such is the correspondence found in one of his more familiar books, *Letters to a Young Poet*.

In the first letter Rilke responds to the young poet's questions, "Am I any good? Should I be a poet?"

> You ask whether your verses are good. You ask me. You have asked others before. You send them to magazines. You compare them with other poems, and you are disturbed when certain editors reject your efforts. Now I beg you to give all that up. You are looking outward, and that above all you should not do now. Nobody can counsel and help you, nobody. There is only one single way. Go into yourself. Search for the reason that bids you write; find out whether it is spreading out its roots in the deepest places of your heart, acknowledge to yourself whether you would have to die if you were denied to write. This above all — ask yourself in the stillest hour of your night: must I write?

This is the question for you: What *must* you do? What is it that drives you? What do you want to do to fulfill your greatest calling? You are created uniquely — not better than anyone else, just unique. My wife and I once did a seminar entitled "You Are Unique, Just Like Everybody Else." This simply means that in order to live a fulfilling life, you would do well to identify the truly distinctive you.

THE PINNACLE OF SELF-UNDERSTANDING

St. Teresa of Avila said spiritual maturity begins with a true under-standing of one's self. A false or skewed view of self gets in the way of both growth and contentment because it is not founded on reality. I can think of no harder and yet more interesting pursuit than that of self-knowledge. But keep in mind that self-understanding for its own sake is also futile. We seek to know ourselves more fully in order to love better, to serve better, and to reap richer personal rewards.

A good thing isn't always a right thing.

Self-understanding starts with an evaluation process in three areas: our assets, our liabilities, and our values.

KNOW YOUR ASSETS

In the last chapter I told you about Dennis, who, at the age of thirty-two, discovered "who he was." And it was the discovery of "who he was" that led him to be a boat builder. But at the core of Dennis is not a boat builder. Instead, at Dennis' core rests all of the talents, skills, values, and interests that it takes to be a boat builder. It's important that you catch the difference. Your specific job or career does not define the "core you." Your talents, skills, values, interests, and personality define the "core you."

Here's the reason I make the distinction. You have a whole shopping list of skills and interests, and there are scores of jobs and careers and hobbies you can pursue with that shopping list. Dennis, for instance, has a *talent* for working with his hands; he has honed a *skill* for design; he has a *value* for working outside and an *interest* in the sea; and he has an introverted *personality,* which permits him to work for long periods without having to interact with people.

But boat building was not Dennis' only career choice. Dennis might also have pursued carpentry, architecture, or engineering — all in a location near the ocean. Maybe he also enjoyed working with youth. If so, he could have been involved with a group like the Sea Scouts. Building boats is one of Dennis' best matches, but it is not his *only* one.

I use five categories for understanding personal assets: talents, skills, values, interests, and personality. These five categories help you define the resources you bring to the table whenever you consider any endeavor.

Natural Talents
You do scores of things naturally well. Maybe you're good at sports or writing or dealing with detail or even listening. These abilities are natural talents, abilities you were born with, gifts from God at birth. Perhaps your parents even noticed them when you were very young.

Although you can nurture and develop your talents, these are the abilities that come to you *naturally.* You will be particularly strong in these areas without having to work really hard, and you will generally enjoy using these abilities. Dozens of talents fall into the following categories.

- Communication Talents
- Leading/Managing Talents
- Planning Talents
- Organizing Talents

- Coordinating Talents
- Dealing with Data Talents
- Building Talents
- Teaching Talents

Identifying your talents will be one of the most useful exercises you can do because when you focus your efforts on things you like to do and do well, there is a proportionate likelihood of long-term satisfaction.

It's not hard to identify your natural talents. Just ask yourself three questions:

1. What sorts of things do I do really well? (speaking, thinking, writing, working with numbers, building, creating, singing?)

2. What sorts of things do I really enjoy? Maybe it's a repeat of the first list; maybe you'll think of something new.

3. If I showed my list to friends or colleagues, would they agree?

Skills

Skills are attributes for which you have *developed* a proficiency. They may or may not be natural talents. The easiest way to tell the difference between a skill and a natural talent is to examine the level of enjoyment you feel from using it. Some things you do well leave you feeling quite drained, and you wouldn't particularly look forward to doing them again. When this is so, you are most likely identifying a skill rather than a natural talent.

One of my clients is an attorney and was quite good at corporate law. Notice I said "was." Although Sue had developed excellent skills for law, she derived little joy from it. The type of law Sue practiced required only small amounts of people contact, something she loved.

Sue decided to make a change and arranged to get an internal transfer to Human Resources, a department structured around taking care of people. But she discovered Human Resources to be equally dissatisfying. So Sue got one more transfer, this time to a negotiation team. Her job description now calls for her to use more of her natural talents than her skills. By using her training in law and her talent for logic, she wins valuable contracts for her company. And since she functions as part of a development team, she has an opportunity to maximize her talents for working with people. As Sue discovered, there is substantial benefit to understanding the distinction between skills and natural talents.

Values

Have you ever taken a few moments to write down what you believe? It is not only rewarding, but clarifying. It helps you understand why you make certain decisions, why you are excited about certain things, and why other circumstances upset you. Writing down what you believe is a great way to begin clarifying your deep and driving personal values.

Here's one attempt I made several years ago: "I believe that life is a story, told in the form of tragedy, comedy, and fairy tale. It is tragic because sorrow and pain play no favorites; it is comedic because joy arrives in the most unlikely packages at the most unexpected times; and it is fairy tale because hope cannot be thwarted: Frogs will turn into princes, ugly ducklings will become swans. There will always be a bright tomorrow." I owe much to Frederick Buechner's book *Telling the Truth* for crystallizing these fundamental beliefs.

These statements represent the kinds of beliefs I base my life on. In other words, these are some of my personal values. Values function like a personal barometer, giving off signals when you are in or out of sync with your core. They are generally based on a whole set of fundamental human characteristics such as honesty, integrity, truthfulness, and humility. You, however, have your own set of values that are probably not identical to anyone else's. Maybe you place a high value on sacrificial giving; maybe you value hard work; or maybe you value family.

Your values dominate both your attitude and your actions. Here's an example. Most people in North America have two affiliations that reveal their values more than anything else: politics and religion. Your deep-seated values play a major role in the formation of your political affiliations and in the practice of your faith. And it's for that reason people say, "You can't talk about politics and religion." Because your values are so deeply represented, an argument against your political or religious beliefs is not merely esoteric, it's against *you*.

That is why the cost of compromising your personal values is so high. To go against your values can create such an inner conflict that the effect is part and parcel with a personality split. How many times have you met someone who lives one life while believing another? It will inevitably take a heavy toll, one which results in massive guilt or total deconstruction of the values system. Either way the price can be too high.

In the following chapter you will learn a few ways to clarify what your values are.

Interests

While values drive the way you behave, interests drive the activities you enjoy. And, of course, the options are unlimited. Your interests reflect your areas of passion. I know people with an interest in shopping and finding the best deal. Other interests could be reading, gardening, sailing, movies, designing, sports, painting, surfing, sewing, backpacking, or studying.

It may seem I am delving into the realm of the all too obvious, but I have met bunches of people who say they aren't much interested in anything. After some probing we generally find several areas or activities the person enjoys. What is important for you is to identify clearly the kinds of activities you are interested in and enjoy, and to designate time to do them. When you discover a way to intermingle your interests, values, and talents, you will find a highly rewarding endeavor.

When I was twenty years younger, I could identify a greater distinction between my interests and my values. I "had the time" to do things I was merely interested in. But today I find the only things that interest me are those which I deeply value. It is as if time is catching up, and I can spend my precious time only on those few things that matter.

Personality

Consider the following four questions:

- Are you energized by being with other people, or are you revived only by solitude?

- Do you like to "live in the now," being very conscious of what is going on around you, or do you tend to have your head in the clouds, always thinking about tomorrow?
- Do you make decisions based on logic and data, or do you "go with your gut"?
- Do you prefer to have your day structured and orderly, or do you like to keep things flexible, allowing for lots of spontaneity?

You just took a personality test — a horribly abbreviated version of the MBTI (Myers-Briggs Type Indicator), which asks approximately one hundred and twenty such questions. I love the MBTI and use it regularly because it measures four areas of life: (1) how you get energized, (2) how you process information, (3) how you make decisions, and (4) how you organize your life.

The purpose of understanding personality is to see how you approach life. It tells you why some things (like punctuality) are important to you, but may not be as important to someone else. It also indicates your preferred style or approach to life so you can maximize your efforts.

For instance, I have a tendency toward introversion; I require solitude in order to get recharged. Therefore, if I don't regularly schedule "alone times," I do myself harm. I need it to get through another day.

The five areas just described — natural talents, skills, values, interests, and personality — are the rudimentary elements of a PAA, a Personal Asset Assessment. A PAA will be one of the bases for creating a personal plan of action. What might your PAA look like?

• How would you describe your natural talents? Which would make your Top Five?

• What skills have you developed?

• Most importantly, how would you describe your core values? What are those beliefs you cannot compromise?

• And finally, what is your current assessment of your interests and your personality?

Take a couple of minutes to answer these questions and identify some of your talents, skills, values, interests, and personality — your assets.

KNOW YOUR LIABILITIES

I love the duties of pastoring which call for the study of Scripture, commitment to prayer, and the pursuit of spiritual direction. I also love many of the associated responsibilities — weddings, baptisms, creating programs, speaking, writing, counseling, training, and mentoring.

But in spite of my love for pastoring, it appears that, at least for now, I am not built to be a pastor. There are too many liabilities for me. I find the politics of church to be too restricting. I don't work well with boards. Resources are terribly limited. An inordinate amount of time must be devoted to administrative detail. For me, the concept of congregational government is overwhelming — too many people want to tell me how to do my job. (As a result of knowing this, I thank God for the men and women he has granted the grace to bear these burdens for the sake of the church.)

Do you realize how important it is for me to understand this? It breaks my heart, but it has saved my sanity. I love the basic job description of a pastor. In fact, in the last two years I have seriously considered returning. But recognition of the liabilities for me has, in the end, prevailed. At least for now, it is wiser for me to continue my services outside the format of church or parish work.

You can't become anything you want, but you're always capable of more than you could ever become.

Just as you must have a sound understanding of your assets, you must honestly recognize your liabilities. What are the social, environmental, and organizational structures you simply cannot live with? And in which talent and skill areas are you significantly weak? Tremendous dissatisfaction can occur when you don't identify those ever-present liabilities.

I created an instrument for people in job search which analyzes job dissatisfaction potential as well as job satisfaction potential. The test begins by asking questions like, What drives you absolutely crazy in a work environment? Is it micro-management? Bureaucracy? A low level of collegiality? You need to know. If you don't recognize these liabilities and make the appropriate corrections, you won't perform well, and you will be very dissatisfied with your efforts.

Another important dimension of knowing your liabilities is knowing your moral and relational weaknesses. Take me, for example. I'm opinionated. In fact, sometimes I express my opinions so strongly that others are reticent to voice opposite ideas. And I have a very low tolerance for incompetence. If a colleague is expected to complete a project and doesn't follow through, I show my frustration. Plus I get angry too quickly at times. I'll get short with my wife and my son. As you can probably guess, the list could go on.

You, too, have moral and relational weaknesses, perhaps a bunch of them. They may include a bit of greed, with a little envy. Add in some unwarranted anger, top it off with a healthy dose of pride, and you've got quite a mess. What you've got is the same disease everybody else on this planet has. It's called sin.

Sin has become such a taboo subject today, even in churches. And it's a shame. By dismissing the subject, we only further empower sin to do its dastardly deeds. Sin makes us angry, frustrated, and confused. It makes us look outwardly at problems — always blaming and seeing others at fault — when if we just looked inside, we might be able to deal with it.

There is great freedom in knowing, naming, and owning our sins. Let me explain. When we admit our sin (we recognize it, identify it, and take responsibility for it), we are in harmony with our true human nature; sin is part of being human. In John's first letter he writes, "If we claim to be without sin, we deceive ourselves and the truth is not in us." The freeing power begins with acknowledgment. At South Coast Community Church we had a slogan that was a takeoff on Tom Harris' *I'm Okay, You're Okay*. Ours was, "I'm not okay; you're not okay; but that's okay." When everyone admitted it, it was quite freeing.

The greatest freedom, however, is described in another of John's writings. In his gospel John quotes Jesus, "You will know the truth and the truth will set you free." The truth Jesus speaks is that you and I have sin. We mess up on a regular basis. Our motives are frequently selfish and impure. Instead of loving, we wish bad things for other people.

The truth that sets you free is that your sin is no surprise to anyone (believe me, just ask a friend), but more importantly, it is no surprise to God. That's why Jesus came to earth in the first place, to remove our guilt and to empower us to reduce our tendency to continue doing those things we have named as sins. To free us from ourselves.

KNOW YOUR VALUE

The third element of honest self-understanding is knowing your inherent human value, that you are lovable and that you are loved.

This is a hard one because deep inside each of us is a nasty little voice that keeps telling us we are not worth the love someone may offer, or that we don't deserve it. It's like the old Rodney Dangerfield line, "I'd never date a woman who would go out with a guy like me." When it comes to loving and being loved, we tend to have a low view of our worthiness.

Once, when I was on retreat with the pastoral staff at South

Coast, we did an affirmation exercise in which the ten pastors were asked to express two things they appreciated about each of the other pastors. One of the pastors, Joe Hemphill, was a mountain of a man of God. He had ministered in churches for more than thirty-five years, devoting his life to God and people. When it came Joe's turn to listen to nine other guys tell him why he was appreciated, he sat there and wept. After the last guy spoke, Joe said, "I've been in ministry thirty-five years, and I have never felt this much appreciation."

My friend Joe found it difficult to listen to people praise him. But he's not alone. Since then, I've done this exercise scores of times, and without exception people feel incredibly awkward receiving praise. Watching them, you would get the impression that listening to a litany of personal praise is a painful experience. And for many of us it is. We simply don't believe it. Or "we know better." We say something like, "Oh, I'm really not that good at... Here's why." Somewhere deep inside we just don't believe such affirmations could be true.

You are unique, just like everybody else.

The truth of the matter is that, in spite of what you may believe, you are loved. You have family, friends, colleagues, and coworkers. People really do care very deeply about you. Even if you don't think so. Even if you are an ornery, cantankerous curmudgeon. There are people who see through your pain and love you for it. Just look around.

There is another source of love for you, and that is God. Even if you refuse to believe that God loves you, it makes no difference. He loves you anyway. No matter who you are. You can't earn it because, as a friend of mine is fond of saying, "Jesus loves you for no good reason." In *Embracing the Love of God*, James Bryan Smith writes, "What we long to know is that we are loved. To be more specific, we hunger to know that we are accepted as we are, forgiven for what we have done, and cared for by a gracious, loving God. When we know this we walk away well."

IN TUNE

Where are you on the trek up the slopes to the pinnacle? How well do you know your assets? Have you honestly evaluated and reckoned with your liabilities? Do you really believe in your inherent and immutable value? And finally, do you find yourself living accordingly?

Living consistently with our internal workings has become increasingly difficult in our busy and demanding society. So many people and organizations tempt us to live outside our own strength and purpose and desires. Therefore, above anything else the reinvented life requires a high commitment to personal integrity. Integrity begins with cognizance of who we really are — all of the aspects discussed in this chapter. But beyond cognizance is the consistent honoring of that self-understanding. Shakespeare nailed it when he wrote in *Hamlet*, "To thine own self be true." Integrity is the result of staying "in tune" with your assets.

In the movie *Rob Roy*, the character of Rob Roy is asked by his son, "Father, what is honor?" Rob Roy tells him, "Honor is something no man can give to you and no man can take away. Honor is a man's gift to himself."

What you "must" do isn't necessarily a "must-do."

In this case, honor and integrity are used synonymously. Integrity, like honor, cannot be bestowed upon you. It can only come from yourself. And when you give it to yourself, everyone knows. It's obvious. You have a relaxed confidence and an unshakable security because you have an integrity that comes from a devout belief in yourself, in your God-given abilities, and even more importantly, in the trustworthiness of your God who both supersedes and empowers all of your assets.

A life of personal integrity is in large measure a matter of holding true to your assets. It is understanding your values and refusing to compromise them. In an article in *USA Today*, Michael Jordan was asked, "Why is it that you've never been close to being the highest paid player in the league, yet you've never had a contract dispute or ever demanded to renegotiate?"

Michael Jordan's response is worthy of our admiration. He said, "I've always honored my word.... People said I was underpaid, but when I signed on the dotted line, I gave my word." A perfect example of an inner integrity expressed outwardly.

It's not always so easy to be a woman or man of integrity. You have daily temptations to compromise, temptations in the form of money, power, and fame. Sometimes it's just a whole lot easier to compromise. But remember the eternal truth: Easy things give immediate joy but generally offer longer-term pain, while hard things bring immediate pain with longer-term satisfaction and joy.

Knowing your most valuable possessions — your assets, your liabilities, and your value — is the first, necessary step to a life of purpose. Living according to them is the second, most rewarding step.

Significant self-reinvention requires significant self-assessment. Without it you run the risk of "living someone else's life." And, as you will discover in the next chapter, a good understanding of self is vital for creating the future as you want it to be.

Right Turns

RECALL THE RIGHT IDEAS

- Self-understanding begins with three areas of knowledge: our assets, our liabilities, and our value. These create our "core."
- Our assets include five distinct areas: natural talents, learned skills, values, interests, and personality.
- Liabilities are as critical as assets. Learning what we aren't helps us discover what we are.
- It's tempting to live outside our own strength, purpose, and desires. That's why a reinvented life requires a high commitment to personal integrity.

DECIDE WHAT'S RIGHT FOR YOU

- Which of your learned skills do you use and value most?
- What natural talent are you most proud of and why?
- How can your liabilities actually help keep you on the right track?
- How many of your talents, values, and liabilities do you attribute to genetics?

MAKE THE RIGHT MOVES

- Write a page describing yourself as if you were trying to acquaint a stranger with this person quickly. For example, "Let me tell you about Derek..." How hard is this exercise for you?
- Two things that seem at odds with one another are often both true about us. List several of these "personal paradoxes." For example, "I am very friendly but also quite shy."
- Plan small activities each week that strengthen your assets in some way. Take a class, read on a subject that fascinates you, call a certain friend, take a walk to pray.
- Make it a habit at night to review your day with an eye to integrity. "Did I live my life today consistently with who I am?"

As long as you don't know where you're going
it doesn't matter where you are.

A P O C R Y P H A L

The mind of man plans his way, but the LORD directs his steps.

P R O V E R B S   1 6 : 9 ,   N A S B

CHAPTER SIX

DREAMSTARTS

I n the past decade or so, corporations all over the world have come to recognize the value of longer-range strategic planning. They ask themselves, "Beyond making a ton of money, who do we want to be? What is our core business? How can we improve and expand? What is our ultimate vision, and how do we plan to get there?" It's a process that is changing the face of business.

My job as a consultant in corporations is to assist teams — all levels of teams, from management to production to staff — in the development of their plans. In the past few years it has occurred to me, that if strategic planning is so profitable for business, why don't we implement the same planning in our personal lives? Just as businesses allocate millions of dollars each year to strategic planning, I believe that each of us individually would do well to spend a few hours considering not only "who we want to be," but "*how* we plan to get there."

DREAMS AND ASPIRATIONS

Kevin works for an engineering firm and for years has not really enjoyed his work. Recently he has been dreaming about pursuing the field of gardening and landscape architecture. Kevin's natural talents for creative gardening are obvious. The gardens he planned and planted around his home are a highlight to passersby who regularly stop to inquire who did the design.

Ordinarily Kevin would have disregarded his dreams as wishful thinking, but he recently learned he may receive a blessing in disguise. His number may be up in the corporate downsizing process, forcing him to consider alternative employment opportunities. (Many times the task of personal reinvention is forced on us, and it can indeed be a blessing in disguise.) Given his new circumstances Kevin is planning to use his severance package for ongoing education in his new field. And within a couple of years, his dream of gardening and landscape architecture may be a reality.

I believe in dreams like Kevin's. Dreams and aspirations are everything. They represent your core, your greatest gifts as well as your greatest needs. They resonate with your most intimate parts and inform you about who you need to be. Dreams offer you direction, and no one ever succeeded without a clearly understood direction.

When I say "dreams," I mean dreams in the fullest sense of the word. Pictures formed in your brain (usually your "right brain") that represent a desired future state. Not every dream is the kind that directs your future, but no vision of the future is complete without a dream. For most of us these kinds of dreams occur while we're awake, in a kind of "daydream" where we imagine and hope for a more ideal state. However, for many people important messages also come while they sleep.

I'm an overly active dreamer. I dream in multicolor, CD-quality, stereophonic abstractions. But like many people, my dreams usually occur in broad daylight and at the craziest times. For instance, I can be chatting with a client when all of a sudden I get a clear picture of a strategy or plan or tool.

Some of you are thinking, "I'm glad for you, but I'm not a dreamer. It's just not me." And to that I say, "Baloney." Everyone is a dreamer. It's impossible not to be. You dream about your life regularly. You imagine how you intend to redecorate that family room or what your next car will look like or how you will shoot the winning shot in the next game of hoops or how your boss will respond to your request or how your gourmet meal will look.

DREAMSHOTS

Creating dreams about significant living is something you can make happen on purpose. Such dreams provide one of the starting points for reinvention. Unfortunately most people fail to give credence to their dreams, laughing them off as wishful thinking. I think that's tragic. Taking the necessary risks to accomplish your dreams may be a little scary, but certainly not prohibitive.

All your dreams and longings are vital, even the illogical ones — maybe especially the illogical ones — because your dreams are trying to reveal to you very important pieces of who you are. Your dreams — about career, God, relationships, family, possessions, peace, simplicity — are snapshots of your soul. They inform you of missing pieces, necessary changes, and true potential. These visual snapshots, when placed together in a giant "dream collage," create a composite mural of who you are created to be.

The best dreams are always a little unreasonable, but not quite impossible.

You have thousands of these snapshots: snapshots of family, kids, service, career, worship, houses, and cars. All of these inform you of your needs and desires. Now certainly, some of these snapshots ought to be tested. A great test is your Personal Asset Assessment (chapter 5). How well do your dreams fit into your mix of talents, skills, values, interests, and personality?

If your dreams of a future state occur in slumber, consider a potentially powerful source for those dreams. If dreams are snapshots of your soul, then it is no wonder we find in Scripture God frequently speaking through dreams. The Book of Job says, "For God does speak — now one way, now another — though man may not perceive it. In a dream, in a vision of the night, when deep sleep falls on men as they slumber on their beds, he may speak in their ears."

In dreams and visions God spoke to Jacob, Pharaoh, Daniel, Joseph, Mary, Paul, John, and others. Whether sleeping or awake, these visionaries were offered guidance from God, who speaks to us in all kinds of ways, sometimes gently, sometimes harshly, through dreams and visions and everyday life. It would be wise to pay heed.

DARING TO DREAM

Impossible things almost always begin with a crazy dreamer: Apple Computer with a teenage Steve Jobs, a colorblind society with Dr. Martin Luther King Jr., a round earth with Christopher Columbus, a light bulb with Thomas Edison, love and medical care for the needy with Mother Teresa. The list could fill this book.

And every time a dreamer fulfills a dream, someone will call it a miracle, but it's not. It's merely a dream that a person had the courage or audacity to pursue. In *Apollo 13*, Buzz Aldren says of Neil Armstrong's walk on the moon, "It wasn't a miracle. We just decided to do it."

How about you? What is it that you have "just decided to do"? What are your dreams? And what does your "dream collage" reveal?

If you're not sure of your dreams, don't be surprised. We live in the midst of a great cultural irony. On the one hand, we're told that nothing is impossible and that we should pursue our greatest dreams.

But on the other hand, if we convey to someone an admirable dream, we're likely to be laughed at and even rejected for having dreams that are out of the ordinary.

You might need reconditioning so you can actually dare to dream. Maybe you need to be a bit "unreasonable" and give yourself permission to dream. It is not only okay for you to dream, it is necessary.

THE ART OF STEERING

No matter how well-planned and how well-defined your goal is, it will be different when you get there. Circumstances and desires change, and so do you. But more importantly, God redirects. I really believe the proverb, "The mind of man plans his way, but the LORD directs his steps."

You might imagine your life as a raft going down a long river. When the current is gentle and the water smooth, it's easy to control your raft. If you're not careful, you'll soon be lulled into believing that life itself is pretty easy. But, at some uncertain time you will hit the rapids and white water. Before long, you realize the river is in control, not you. That's when you learn "to steer through" the rapids, rather than "master" them.

Significant living is more about the art of steering, than the tedious task of mastering. You prepare, you plan, you strategize, and then you go out and take it as it comes.

In another book I referred to this as "God-room." It's good for us to know that life is always just a bit out-of-control. It keeps us sharp — and humble, dependent on an all-knowing God. In a New Testament letter James writes, "Now listen, you who say, 'Today or tomorrow we will go to this or that city, spend a year there, carry on business and make money.' Why, you do not even know what will happen tomorrow.... Instead, you ought to say, 'If it is the Lord's will, we will live and do this or that.'"

My grandmother's Oklahoma version was "We'll be there — Lord willing and the creek don't rise."

DREAMSTARTS

Most people would agree that great accomplishments generally begin with a dream, many times a crazy dream. But what most people don't know is that the next step to realizing the dream is *not* the plan. In the creative dreaming process there is an interesting intermediate step between the vision and the plan — the *articulation* of the vision.

Vision ————> Verbalization ————> Plan

Verbalizing a dream actually helps it happen. By merely stating your dream on a regular basis, you unconsciously give yourself both power and permission to accomplish it. It also provides you the opportunity to receive valuable feedback from other people. As you continue on the road of reinvention, I encourage you to find co-adventurers, supportive people who are willing to listen to your dreams with an open mind. But first you need to identify your dreams.

Brent Defosse, a creative manager with Chevron Canada Resources, is a very forward thinker and therefore highly visionary. He loves to tell his direct reports, "When your eyes stay focused on the ground, the journey forward always looks the same." You gotta look up and you gotta look ahead if you expect to do anything of any significance.

A dream always dies without a plan to give it life.

After you've given yourself permission to dream, you need to go the next step and develop your dream. But how? Developing our dreams can be hard, mostly because we are so inexperienced at it. But it's also great fun. I see it as a four-step process:

One: Create Your Vision

Two: Incorporate Your Driving Values

Three: Identify Your Goals

Four: Regularly Measure Your Progress

Let's talk about the steps.

One: Create Your Vision

In my consulting business I am frequently called in to assist management teams in creating operational plans. One of the first things I ask is to see their mission and vision statements, as a way of familiarizing myself with their business. I need to know where they want to go. If they have no mission or vision, I force them to create one. It is vital. All business planning begins with a vision of the end result. The same principle is true for individuals.

A non-negotiable step for you to reinvent your life is to develop a concise statement that embodies your dreams. *A vision is the composite picture of all your dreams.* It is the kind of statement you can look at with pride and say, "Yep. That's me in a nutshell." Although it's a taxing process, it can also be surprisingly simple.

I encourage people to focus their personal vision statements around the Four Ps — passion, purpose, people, and praise. In doing so, they are likely to create a well-rounded and integrated approach to life. Failing to create a vision around the Four Ps could easily lead to disappointment and dissatisfaction because each area or domain is essential for significant reinvention. Note the following scale of benefits...

FOUR Ps	WITH IT YOU HAVE...	WITHOUT IT YOU HAVE...
PASSION	EXCITEMENT	BURN-OUT
PURPOSE	SATISFACTION	FRUSTRATION
PEOPLE	LOVE	LONELINESS
PRAISE	DESTINY	HOPELESSNESS

To initiate your vision-making process, consider questions like...

Passion: How you approach life

What do you love to do?

With what kind of attitude do you approach life?

Purpose: What you want to accomplish

What skills do you love to employ?

What impact do you want to make?

What have you always dreamed of doing?

People: Who and how you plan to love

Whom do you love?

What do you need from your relationships?

Praise: How you plan to worship

Whom do you serve?

How does God desire you to demonstrate love for him?

Sometimes it is difficult to answer these questions. We have so much confusing information and so many other people we're trying to please that identifying our own desires may feel almost impossible.

In my vision-setting and personal-planning workshops, I suggest a fun and revealing exercise to people who are having a hard time answering those questions: If you were to die tomorrow, what would you wish the people closest to you would say about you? What kind of impact would you like to have made on them? Write two or three sentences as if coming from each person.

It's helpful to start with a vision of the end. In the internationally recognized planning process called PERT (Project Evaluation Review Technique), the planner begins the process by first creating an accurate picture of the final scenario. When you look at your life as if you've just died, you're certainly beginning with the end. In a sense you are "PERTing" out your life.

A dream is not something that you wake up from,
but something that wakes you up.

It is not enough, however, to have a vision. Not by a long shot. You also need to identify those values which drive your vision.

Two: Incorporate Your Driving Values

In the previous chapter we introduced the notion of values as internal barometers which guide our behavior. Now, as promised, is the time to offer a few ideas about how to identify your individual values, the kinds of beliefs that govern your direction.

We hear a lot of talk today about values, especially "family values." It seems as if it has become every politician's watchword. However, few attempt to define what those values actually are. And when they do, they are quickly shot down. That is because everyone has a slightly different set of values. We may find large areas of similarity, but there will always be significant differences.

Each of us has a whole set of values that ultimately determine how we judge goodness and badness, and how we decide what is right and wrong. If we are not careful, however, circumstances in life can erode our values by encouraging us to chip away at our beliefs. For instance, very few people would condone robbery, but how many billions of dollars are lost each year to software theft?

More people define themselves by their problems than by their dreams.

I encourage clients to make a list of five to ten fundamental values. The following questions can begin to help you identify your core values.

Whom do you respect, and what are their respectable qualities?
What do you want God to say about you the first time you meet face to face?
What would the ideal society be like?
What qualities would you want your kids to espouse?

Remember, you function best and happiest when your behaviors reflect your values, and when they don't, you feel sorely out of line with your truest self.

Three: Identify Your Goals

It is not enough to have a vision and values. You also need some way of identifying successes and areas for improvement. Visions and dreams have to be translated into goals, both long-term and short-term. Long-term goals look ahead five to twenty years and are closely aligned with your vision. But in my opinion, short-term goals are where you should devote most of your energy.

All significant progress occurs "incrementally," one step at a time. I am a giant advocate of setting short-term goals that are realistic, as well as a stretch. These goals must be both doable and measurable. I stress the qualifiers "doable" and "measurable." It makes no sense to create goals you know you won't reach, like "I will exercise five days a week" when you have as yet to find the energy to exercise five days a month. Instead, set a goal to exercise a couple of times each week and work your way up.

Here are some questions you might consider for creating your goals:

What long-term accomplishments would be in place if you had successfully fulfilled your dream?

What do you need to do on an annual basis in order to live according to your dream?

What kinds of things would you like to do this year that would make it a great year?

A sample of *annual* goals might look like this:

Passion: How you approach life
- Read five novels.
- Learn to scuba.
- Walk two times a week.
- Play with my kids.

Purpose: What you want to accomplish
- Get the promotion.
- Save $_____
- Learn the new accounting system.
- Create a new ministry at church.

People: Who and how you plan to love
- Have monthly date nights with my husband.
- Listen to my son.
- Spend two hours a week with my best friend.
- Call my mom weekly.

Praise: How you plan to worship
- Attend church every Sunday.
- Have devotions three times a week.
- Read two spiritual books.
- Find a discipling/mentoring relationship

These "actionable goals" will be the basis for your quarterly review.

Four: Regularly Measure Your Progress
The most common failure I have found with progressive companies and aspiring individuals is not the failure to dream, or to plan, but to measure. The reason few people ever accomplish New Year's resolutions or maintain a diet or exercise program is that they don't measure, regularly.

But, in my personal life, I have a giant problem when it comes to measuring "regularly." I've always thought that time management systems were fairy tales. I'm great at making to-do lists; the problem is I turn around and lose them. I'm doomed to fail at time management because most time management and personal management systems are far too demanding. They expect me to track my work daily or weekly, when I've discovered I can't even keep up monthly.

So I decided to create a personal management system for people like me — one where I managed the system rather than the system managing me.

Here's how I manage annual goals. I take one day at the beginning of the year to review my vision and values. At this time I also create my new annual goals. I sit on the plan for a day or so, then come back to determine if I still like it. If so, I move on. Then once every quarter I measure my progress. By spending only twenty to thirty minutes four times per year, I have realized a radical increase in my personal productivity.

The measurement system is simple. I evaluate my performance in each area on a "+, √, -" system:

"+" = *very good*
"√" = *satisfactory*
"-" = *needs improvement.*

The areas that receive a "√-" or below go onto an improvement list.

Fulfilling a vision never happens by accident. The most successful and most fulfilled people are intentional. They do things on purpose. I fear there is a myth that if you merely write down your vision, it will somehow magically and mysteriously come about. Not true. It requires intention and attention. Martin Luther King Jr., Christopher Columbus, Thomas Edison, and Mother Teresa are all great because they had vision, they had faith, and they had a plan. You will also attain your "greatness," (defined by you) as you set out intentionally.

But please remember one thing about the planning system: A system is always your servant, never your master. Use it to your benefit. When it no longer works, modify it.

SAMPLE PORTFOLIOS

To give you an idea of what a personal vision package might look like, here are two samples of Personal Vision, Values, and Goals. A Personal Portfolio has four sections: (1) Vision Statement; (2) Values Statement; (3) Annual Goals and Tracking System; and (4) Quarterly Improvement Guide.

The first sample is mine, after having refined this over five years. The second sample is from Carol Bruce, an attendee at one of my workshops. Her vision, values, and goals were essentially created in a one-day workshop.

As you review these portfolios, keep in mind that, although they may sound simple, they are deep reflections of a personal identity.

Also remember that these are in response to the question, "When you review your accomplishments at the end of the year, if you did all the things on your list would you call it a *great year*?"

CHARLIE HEDGES' VISION

Passion

I live each day fully; awake and aware of the wonder around me; grateful for the grace I receive and compelled to express that same grace to others. I work (and play) with intensity and comedy, always striving to encourage, have impact, and bring a sense of childlike freshness to the lives of those around me.

Purpose

I nurture and express my talents in order to be an effective agent of grace, hope, strategic direction, and personal development. I work to contribute to the support and well-being of my family and my home. I am continuously self-improving, not for the sake of achievement but for understanding and meaningful service.

People

I practice love of God, family, and friends. My love and commitment to Pam is unique, for she alone has my lifelong oath of love before God. My love for my son is also unique in that he is our creative gift of God. I am deeply committed to a handful of friends who fill my life with wisdom, humor, and love.

Praise

I regularly focus my love and attention on God, the creator and sustainer of all life. It is through his mystery, grace, and goodness that I find power and contentment.

VALUES

I believe in and value…

1. Grace

   Treasure life as a gift from God.

   Practice daily the privilege of loving God.

2. Strength/Fortitude

   Be responsible.

   Fight the good fight, hard.

3. Love

   Succeed at home first.

   Embrace people with openness and acceptance.

4. Hope

   Contribute to the felt self-value of others by word and deed.

   Facilitate the growth and success of others.

5. Human Dignity

   Respect the rights and beliefs of others.

   Seek first to understand before passing judgment.

6. Being Real (Integrity)

   Always be real.

   Acquire enough wisdom to be humble.

7. Fun

   Remember to find joy in my labor, for it too is a gift from
      God.

   Have at least one hearty laugh each day.

8. Impact

   Work to make a difference.

   Practice the courage to take risks.

1995 PERSONAL GOALS

RATING	GOAL	JAN-MAR	APR-MAY	JUL-SEPT	OCT-DEC	YEAR END
PASSION						
Fun	Movies/Plays/Concerts	√	√			
	Hiking & parks w/ Austin	+	√			
Read	——— Fiction	√	√			
Health	Eat; Walk; Tennis	√-	√			
PURPOSE						
Financial	Earn $ ———	+	+			
	Save $ ———	+	√-			
Family Plan	Follow it	√	√			
Write	Letter to Terry	-	-			
	New book: Begin contract discussion	√	√			
Read	——— Non-fiction	√-	√			
Home Improvements	Backyard landscape additions	√	√-			
	Austin's room	-	+			

RATING	GOAL	JAN-MAR	APR-MAY	JUL-SEPT	OCT-DEC	YEAR END
PEOPLE						
Family	Love Pam -Help reduce stress— Affirm prof. talents -Make feel secure— Affirm beauty	√	√-			
	-Father Austin, to develop sense of... -Security, Ability -Confidence, Nurture (know he's loved)	+	+			
Nurture Friendships	Level One (Binding) -Steve-Terry-George	+	+			
	Level Two (Intimate) -Todd-Jim-Rich -Audrey-Tom-Denny	√ +	√-			
PRAISE						
Devotional Life	Morning prayer; some evenings	√	√ +			
	Sunday worship	+	+			
	Read Scripture; books on spiritual life	√-	√			

Family Plan   + = very good   √ = satisfactory   - = needs improvement.

CAROL BRUCE'S VISION

Note: Carol is a volunteer at her local church who is about to devote the bulk of her time to single-adult ministries.

Passion
I live each day with a renewed excitement, creating a life of spontaneity for others and myself.

Purpose
In order to be a beacon of light in a world of darkness, I am a role model and a mentor of biblical truth to others. I am available to lead others in crises or need, keeping an open mind while listening to the call for help.

People
I am truthful and honest in relationships with others, creating an intimacy that will foster trust and loyalty to each other.

Praise
I am available to God's plan by communicating with him daily to focus on his will for me personally.

VALUES

1. Intimate Friendship
2. Other People's Needs
3. Integrity
4. Role Model
5. Flexibility / Spontaneity
6. Loyalty
7. Forgiveness

1996 PERSONAL GOALS

RATING	GOAL	JAN-MAR	APR-MAY	JUL-SEPT	OCT-DEC	YEAR END
PASSION						
Relax	Visit sunset/ sunrise 1 time/wk for 1 hr					
	Entertain friend— meal/fellowship 1 time/month					
Exercise	Walk 2 miles 2 times/week					
PURPOSE						
Service	Volunteer @ counseling room					
	Lead DRW's					
	Facilitate Single Again Group					
Study	Visit other SA ministries 1 weekend 2 times/year					
	Send card to encourage people 4 times/month					
Read	Biography of spiritual leader 1 time/quarter					
Mental Health	Limit TV					

RATING	GOAL	JAN-MAR	APR-MAY	JUL-SEPT	OCT-DEC	YEAR END
PEOPLE						
Family	Cyndi:affirm her talents 1 time/wk					
	John: visit in person 1 time/qtr.					
Nurture Friendships	Sherry: meet in person 1 time/mo.					
	Donna: lunch or coffee 1 time/ mo.					
	Pam: lunch or coffee 1 time/mo.					
	Janet: walk the trail 2 times/mo.					
PRAISE						
Devotional Life	Listen to praise tapes in my car					
	Journal prayers each Sat. A.M.					
	Study spiritual devotions book 1 time/month					
	Retreat for silence & solitude 1 time/qtr.					

Family Plan   + = very good   √ = satisfactory   - = needs improvement.

Right Turns

RECALL THE RIGHT IDEAS

- Just as businesses allocate millions to strategic planning, each of us should invest time considering *who* we want to be and *how* we plan to get there.
- Creating dreams about significant living is something we can and should do on purpose.
- Our dreams and longings are vital, especially the illogical ones, because they reveal important pieces of who we are.
- Taking the necessary risks to accomplish our dreams is scary. Often, verbalizing our dreams to others helps bring them into being.

DECIDE WHAT'S RIGHT FOR YOU

- How "reasonable" does dreaming feel to you in light of your present circumstances?
- What dreams have come true in your life already? What dreams were put on a shelf, and why?
- What do you see as the number one barrier to your most desired dream?
- Who do you know whose crazy dreams came true?

MAKE THE RIGHT MOVES

- Describe on paper what your wildest dream would look like at a glance: "I'm sitting at a TV news studio desk…"

- Think through what your dreams say about you. What would you make of a person who dreamed your dreams?
- Incorporate your dreams into your prayers, asking God to show you a destiny and inviting his guidance.
- Keep a dream list in your notebook that you refer to and add to from time to time.

PART THREE

Revamping Your Strategies

Putting change in action

Your thinking is right, and you have taken steps to know yourself and to know your dreams. Now let's do something with it.

Self-reinvention almost never happens by accident. It takes a purposeful and intentional approach. Three timeless strategies will greatly assist you in the reinventing process.

Prosperity will have its season; and even when it's here, it's going by.

DAVID WILCOX
FROM *ALL THE ROOTS GROW DEEPER*
BIG HORIZON CD

Crowds of people came to hear him and to be healed of their sicknesses.
But Jesus often withdrew to lonely places and prayed.

LUKE 5:15-16

CHAPTER SEVEN

STABLE CHANGE

Billie Mae Abernathy entered this world in 1920, the sixth of ten children born to Bascom and Lela Abernathy, sharecroppers in the tiny Oklahoma town of Bokchita. Years later Billie Mae would watch Johnnie Cash on TV as he reminisced about the "good ole days" back on the farm. "That man either has a bad memory or has never worked on a farm," she would say. "There's no such thing as the good ole days on the farm! Farm work is long and it's hard."

In those days farm kids grew up, went to school, started farming, and then kept on farming. That's the way it was and the way it was supposed to be. But Billie Mae had other ideas. By the time she was twelve years old, she swore she would get off that farm. And when she graduated from high school, she said good-bye, left, and got a job in the big city of Albuquerque, New Mexico. From that day forward she worked in the city and sent money back home to help her family.

Billie Mae was a pioneer. She broke the rules. You weren't supposed to leave the farm. That's where your security was — family was on the farm, food was on the farm, your home was on the farm. You belonged on the farm. But Billie Mae did the unthinkable. She left. And she made it. She went first, and later every brother and sister would follow. She set straight the path for her siblings, and for my sister and me.

Billie Mae was my mom. And as a pioneer, she taught me one of the key secrets of living adventurously — creating a stable environment from which to make your changes. Great change is best bred on stable ground.

As you've been reading this book, chances are you've identified a few new adventures of your own, some opportunities and challenges you'd like to undertake. Or possibly you have some old habits or "wrong rules" you want to get rid of. Perhaps you don't feel like you have the kind of circumstantial stability right now to make the changes you'd like. Maybe you're thirty-five years old and want to go back to school in order to change careers, but you have low cash flow and your wife's sister just moved in.

Major change is always a pretty scary option. For the reinventing person, however, there is *no* other way. Self-reinvention, by definition, demands that you alter behaviors and environments. But how?

In chapter one we looked at the *edge of chaos theory*, which describes how life is played out on a stage of constant tension between stability and change. You *need* stability. You also *need* change because without it you lose vibrancy. What's more, there is a dynamic relationship between stability and change: Change occurs best in a stable environment. When you understand this relationship between stability and change, you will discover a new source of power.

The moment you start to change you want to stop it.

Without knowing the chaos theory, Billie Mae understood this fundamental truth: Change is good, but it's easiest and most productive when it evolves from a secure place. As a pioneer herself, my mom formed in me the belief that I could regularly "go against the grain." But she also provided a safe and loving environment in which my adventuresome spirit could readily find peace and security. Every night we ate dinner as a family; we always shared household chores equally; we spent every vacation together; we never ceased kissing and hugging; and we made it a habit to encourage risk and to learn from failure — all of which promote security and stability.

THE INSECURITY OF SECURITY

One of life's great ironies is that, in spite of our natural proclivity for change, we have an equally natural proclivity to resist it. We have innate fears that drive us to pursue stability and security, which are also healthy pursuits. The problem is that most of the time we look for security in "external things" that are inherently insecure — jobs, houses, possessions, and even marriages.

In reality, you have little control over these areas. They can change even when you do everything right. You know this is true because you've seen or experienced the tragic failure of supposedly secure things: families who based their retirement on the stock market and lost half of their monthly income due to a drastic drop in interest rates; friends who landed the perfect job and then lost it for some unforeseeable reason; people who met the mate of their dreams only to discover the dream was really a nightmare in disguise; friends who planned the perfect engagement, listened to all the premarital counseling, attended church regularly, had their 2.5 kids, and ten years later divorced.

What looks safe is not always secure.

No matter how secure you think you are today, tomorrow could be very different. In 1972 Richard Nixon won the presidency by the second greatest landslide in election history; eighteen months later he was forced to leave office in disgrace. In 1991 George Bush attained one of the highest approval ratings in the history of the US presidency (65 percent); one year later he was defeated by Bill Clinton. Many of today's staunch conservatives were once long-haired hippies promoting social democracy and swearing they would never align themselves with the establishment.

Okay. Change is inevitable. It is also necessary for success. And we agree that change happens best in stable and secure conditions. We even agree that little security can be found in jobs, houses, cars, or even some people. Where, then, can you find your stability?

Ultimately, all stability and security rest in the hands of God. Although he dispenses his security in a loving and wise manner, he also does it mysteriously. No one knows the mind of God, but in his providence he has provided us a number of alternatives for creating our own inner security. Oddly enough, *you* are the stable place from which you can best make changes. But you must help *you* in getting there.

LITURGICALLY ALIVE

Change occurs in two ways: on purpose, or by accident. When it happens on purpose, you are prepared because you've likely created the stability from which it spawns. When it happens by accident, it is always more painful and frequently less productive. And for most of us, that's how change seems to happen most often. How can we reverse that tendency?

Several years ago when I began my retreats to a Benedictine monastery, I was introduced to the routines of living in a religious order. The monks who live in this community of faith wake at the same hour daily and retire at the same hour nightly. They pray five times each day at the same hour, they eat at the same hour, study at the same hour, and work at the same task at the same hour. They even have their "free time" at the same hour — every day, every month, every year.

To the rest of us, the monastic lifestyle might sound like a nightmare. What about freedom? What about spontaneity? What about individuality? What about creativity?

During my first encounter, I had difficulty identifying with this liturgical or regulated lifestyle because it seemed so restrictive. But as time wore on, I began to recognize the value. My understanding has steadily evolved so that today, oddly enough, I live what might be called a mini-liturgical (regulated) lifestyle. It's nothing like the discipline of the monks, but liturgical nevertheless. For me, this means I do certain things that I love on a regular, daily basis.

My liturgical habits consist of rising early each day. I exercise, pray, ponder Scripture, and putz about in my garden — a sixty- to ninety-minute process. Every day the same thing, except Wednesday and Sunday when my prayer time is at church. Every day, every day, every day. To my delight I have discovered that not only is it *not* boring, it has become essential! I depend on those few moments of rest and redemption.

One of my greatest discoveries since committing to a daily pattern has been an increase in creativity. After the first few months I had more new and fresh ideas than I'd had in the previous few years. That's because doing what you love — regularly — is a hotbed for passion and change and creativity. You create an environment for stability to increase, which in turn empowers you to make changes and be creative. It becomes the mechanism by which you can take charge of your changes.

Liturgical living is one way to create the kind of stability I've been talking about. But what exactly would be the components of your personal liturgy?

DO WHAT YOU LOVE AND THE REST WILL FOLLOW

First: Do What You Love

This may sound redundant, but what do you love to do? I mean really love to do? I'm talking about those activities or investments of time that you find rewarding, fun, maybe even challenging or difficult; activities that tap into your talents; activities that are refreshing, perhaps exhilarating, or, on the other hand, relaxing; activities that maximize both your spiritual and physical sides, ones that tap into something fundamental and rudimentary in you.

Maybe it's playing a sport, or building something, or getting together with a certain group of friends, or reading or writing or gardening or cooking. Maybe, even...it's your job. Whatever the activity or investment of time may be, when was the last time you did it? And when was the last time before that? And the last time before that? Whatever it is you love to do, you need to do it *regularly*.

According to the Myers-Briggs Type Indicator (MBTI), my friend Tom would be called an introvert. He is energized by ideas and solitude. Therefore, two very enjoyable activities for him are to go to a restaurant alone (but with a good book) and to go to a movie alone. Since his career requires travel, he has ample opportunity to do both. He also loves to read and to be outside. He looks forward to summer when he can take a two-hour lunch and go to the beach. There he sits in a lounge chair, reads a book, and does a little body-surfing. Tom is also the family cook, not because he has to do it but because he loves to. He does all of these things, regularly, with intention.

Perhaps you love to play sports; to write; to paint; to play instruments; to putz around the house, building and repairing. Your options are virtually unlimited. Do what you love, and a host of good things will follow. In her very provocative book *Do What You Love, the Money Will Follow*, Marsha Sinetar very accurately points out that "doing what you love" does not necessarily mean "play." "Doing what you love" can also be work.

Consider the story told of Charles Schulz, creator and illustrator of the popular *Peanuts* comic strip. Since newspapers expect a new *Peanuts* comic every day, Schulz's schedule required that he work for a few hours a day almost every day of the week. It was once pointed out to him that if he were to schedule a couple of months of hard work, he could punch out several comic strips in a short period of time, thereby allowing himself more free time to do those things he wanted to do.

Schulz responded by saying, "You don't get it, do you? Asking me to 'punch out a few comic strips' would be like asking Beethoven to rip off a few symphonies or Rembrandt to dish up a few quick paintings so they could go on about the important things in life." Nonsense. For Schulz, his work *was* what he loved to do.

We live in an age that has devalued work. We treat it as something we must do in order to gain the time to do the things we like to do. Work has become an unpopular but necessary evil. And I guess in some circumstances it is. But it is an unfair generalization when you consider that your work might possibly be one of the truest expressions of your individuality, creativity, and value to society and to yourself.

Again the question is, What do you love to do, and how regularly do you do it? The question is critical because there is a direct correlation between the amount of time you spend doing those things you love to do and the depth of your internal stability.

Two: Incorporate Spiritual Disciplines

I have difficulty with the idea of a "spiritual life." Too often it is portrayed as simply another piece of the jigsaw puzzle of life, such as our work life, our home life, our family life, our emotional life, and our spiritual life. But this kind of talk betrays a radical misunderstanding of our true nature.

We are created in the image of God, to do the works of God, for the benefit of God and his creation. The Holy Spirit oversees our every movement, whether it be at home, at work, at play, or at church. We can do nothing without the Holy Spirit (although, to be sure, a lot of what we do may "grieve" the Spirit). But still, one might say everything we do is spiritual. In the fullest sense, all of life is a spiritual life.

However, in order to keep the spiritual side of yourself vibrant and alive, you need to nurture an acute awareness of contact with God — to know him, talk to him, listen to him, learn about him, and learn from him. The historical route to contact with God is through "spiritual disciplines."

The second, and certainly most foundational, way for you to create a stable hotbed for necessary change, is through developing a rich life of the Spirit. I suggest you do this with the aid of prayer and Scripture. You need only three things: a quiet place, a Bible, and a commitment to a daily routine.

I know the difficulty of committing to any task, let alone prayer, on a daily basis. It has been a giant struggle for me since entering the faith more than fifteen years ago. The solution came, for me, in the form of a prayer book given to me by a friend at a monastery. I discovered that what I needed for my prayer life was more structure. The form of prayer I had been used to was very free and responsive. It called for me to be creative when I needed to be contemplative. My prayer book, *A Shorter Morning and Evening Prayer*, uses the same structure every day: two Psalms, a reading from one of the Major Prophets, a New Testament reading, a couple of hymns, and intercessions. It is all read out loud, and done quickly would take about five minutes; done contemplatively about fifteen. I now look forward to my daily prayers.

I'm not suggesting that you adopt my form of prayer or mode of reading Scripture. What I am suggesting is that you find the way that works for you.

Another way to look at spiritual disciplines is that they are an investment in the stability of God. Philosophers talk about the relationship between *necessary beings* and *contingent beings*. A necessary being is one that needs nothing for survival; it depends wholly upon itself. God is a necessary being. A contingent being is one that requires sustenance from an outside source for survival. We are contingent beings. We depend upon God. In my view, the entire universe is contingent upon God, the ultimate source of life. The amount of time and effort you devote to knowing God and learning from God will correlate directly with the amount of internal stability you have.

Three: Pursue Mental Disciplines

Someone once shared a great quote with me:

Small people talk about people.
Average people talk about things.
Big people talk about ideas.

If talking about people is petty, then talking about ideas is grand. Ideas change the world. Ideas make an impact. Ideas will lead you to significance. Where do "big people" get these ideas? Are they just naturally brilliant? Are ideas just part of their nature? No, ideas come from other ideas. "Big people" get ideas from other people. And they get these ideas from books. "Big people" read!

One of the greatest tragedies to occur in the last fifty years is television — for what it subtly teaches us, but more importantly for what it prevents us from learning and experiencing. Television is taking us on a path of virtual illiteracy. (An excellent discussion of this subject is found in Neil Postman's *The Disappearance of Childhood.*) Because of television's appeal to our need for escape, its addictive nature absorbs all the time we might have otherwise devoted to more useful things, like reading.

Reading is vital for a life of significance. It develops your ability to think critically, to learn widely, and to stretch your horizons. A few months ago I read a statistic on reading that astounded me. In essence it said: If you were to read about one subject for one hour per day for one year, you would be considered an expert on that subject. And if you were to read about one subject for one hour per day for five years, you would be considered in the top 5 percent of experts in the entire world.

I understand that for many folks reading is not so attractive, because I've not always been a reader. For the decade of my twenties I did not read one book. Not one! In fact, I converted from a nonreader to an avid reader when I was around thirty. But, I had to learn to be a reader. And in the last fifteen years I've discovered the joy of reading.

But reading is certainly not the only way to stimulate your mind. You can take classes; learn a hobby; frequent the performing arts; attend city council meetings and a host of other activities. The point is to feed your mind.

A couple of years ago I attended a class on entrepreneurial behaviors by Vance Caesar, an unusually successful entrepreneur. A key point that I grasped from his presentation on business planning was that many new businesses fail because "they don't know what they don't know." Successful entrepreneurs expend a lot of energy trying to discover what they don't know because that will always be a potential gamestopper.

The more we feed our minds, the more we discover what we don't know, and that kind of discovery creates a more stable inner place. Our minds become hotbeds of activity and creativity, anxious for a challenge and secure in their ability to cope.

Four: Learn to Rest

While work is being frequently devalued these days, the whole notion of play is often lifted to a childish state of reverence. There's nothing inherently wrong with play. It is good; it is healthy; it is even necessary. However, more frequently than not, play is synonymous with escape, and escape has very limited value.

The best rest takes work.

We seem to have developed a bipolar culture in which many of us live in two different worlds — the supposed real world, which consists of problems and anxieties regarding careers and families; and the escape world, which consists of denying that "real world" by attempting to "enjoy ourselves."

We have so many modes of escape. Vacations often offer nothing more than a rather dissatisfying and short escape. We take one, two, three, or more weeks, travel to some location that helps us forget our current realities, wait a few days until we can truly "unwind," enjoy the remaining few days, and then return to our normal schedule. But how many days does it take until we are as stressed as when we left? Rarely more than one week.

Perhaps what we need is less escape and more rest. In the contemplative and monastic traditions, there is a critical distinction between rest and escape. Rest, in the contemplative sense, is not necessarily the absence of activity. Rest involves conscious effort. To rest is to put aside; to escape is to avoid. To rest is to recognize; to escape is deny. To rest is to retreat; to escape is to flee.

You rest when you do all the things listed in this section. One of the very best ways you will rest is when you do what you love — even when it might look like a flurry of productivity. Last night I went to a cooking class. I learned how to prepare five new pasta dishes, from perciatelli carbona with pancetta to fusilli with shrimp, roasted garlic, tomatoes, and artichoke hearts. It was great. As soon as class was over, I rushed to the grocery store to buy the ingredients I needed for tonight's meal. I didn't get home until after my normal bedtime, and yet I awoke today refreshed and excited. *I rested with activity* instead of escaping by lying on the couch and watching my favorite sitcom, *Frazier*.

ONCE MORE BILLIE MAE

Billie Mae was my tutor. She instilled within me the spirit of the pioneer and taught me the thrill of the adventure. And she was wise enough to know that the thrill of the adventure, with all its chaotic changes, is built on a hearty dose of internal stability. Without some form of stability, recurrent change can be almost debilitating.

Inner stability is one of those "right things" you'll want to get right because as you will discover next, your reinvention is about to take a risky ride. I've attempted to prepare you for some of the important changes you will plan for yourself. In the next chapter you'll be asked to actually embark on change — which involves risks. Sometimes creating a significant life might require significant risk. The key is to learn how to unrisk the risk.

Right Turns

RECALL THE RIGHT IDEAS

- Change occurs best in a stable environment.
- Our fears about change may drive us to mistakenly pursue stability and security in things we actually have little control over — jobs, houses, possessions, and even marriages.
- Change happens in two ways: on purpose or by accident. On purpose is usually preferable.
- One way to have more control over change is to incorporate liturgical routines into our day, creating stability inside ourselves.

DECIDE WHAT'S RIGHT FOR YOU

- Think back on your life. What were the hardest changes? Did they happen in a stable atmosphere?
- How do you usually respond to unexpected negative changes? Positive ones?

- What is your greatest difficulty when it comes to implementing change? Discouragement? Frustration? Fear of failure? Lack of motivation?
- Is it harder for you to find a way to do what you love, or to figure out what it is you love?

MAKE THE RIGHT MOVES

- Stop right now and list what you've done in the past two days that you love to do. Could any of these be transformed into a regular activity?
- Try to forecast what "weather conditions" you will encounter in your life as you attempt to change. Stormy and unstable? Or too balmy and suffocating? Identify what you can do to create a stable but willing path for change.
- Take a week and incorporate some new spiritual disciplines. Pray every hour for ten minutes, for example. Record your feelings for later reflection. Try to make part or all of this routine a regular part of your "liturgical" lifestyle.
- Write "Stable" and "Changing" at the top of a page. List the activities in your life in the appropriate column. Identify areas of chaos and other areas which might be too stuck. Where are the conflicts?

As long as you think the problem is out there,
that very thought is the problem.

STEPHEN COVEY
FROM *THE 7 HABITS OF HIGHLY EFFECTIVE
PEOPLE*

The LORD had said to Abram, "Leave your country, your people and
your father's household and go to the land I will show you."
… So Abram left.

GENESIS 12:1,4

CHAPTER EIGHT

CALCULATED
RISKS

Have you ever looked back on your life and said, "I wish I had…"?

When I was twenty years old, I was a long-haired, hippie, college drop-out. Along with two other guys, I hitchhiked across the United States and Canada, from Los Angeles to Montreal to New York to the Grand Canyon and back to LA. Three guys, three backpacks, and one guitar; it took ten weeks and four hundred dollars — about thirteen bucks a week each.

Never in my life have I experienced more freedom. We not only lost track of what date it was, but what day of the week it was. The sun came up, the sun went down; it made no difference whether we called it Saturday or Tuesday; it was just another day.

More than once we were given a ride by someone who said, "Boy,

I wish I was doing what you are! Free and on the road." And with the mild arrogance of twenty year olds we would say, "No you don't. If you really wanted to, you'd be doing it." Maybe arrogant. Maybe cocky. But true.

We all have occasions in life when we know what we ought to do, and we don't do it. A career move, or going back to school, or getting married, or pursuing a fascinating avocation. Whatever. One voice inside tells us, "Go for it," and another one says, "Don't be silly. You'd probably fail anyway."

As you journey on the path of self-reinvention, you have to accept an important reality: It will be risky. You will need to undertake new tasks or assume different behaviors that hold the real possibility of failure. Highly successful people understand this reality. But while most risktakers are willing to forgo guarantees, it doesn't mean they haven't calculated the probabilities of success. *Risk taking does not have to mean throwing all caution to the wind and jumping off blindly into some unknown. Risk taking is a calculated, well-planned endeavor.*

Highly successful entrepreneurs who have a reputation for being high-stakes risktakers are actually very careful. According to a statement in *Inc.* magazine, a journal whose target audience is entrepreneurs, "The best entrepreneurs are *risk avoiders.* They identify the risk, and then take actions to minimize the effects of it. When entrepreneurs forget this, they are gamblers at best, and failure statistics at worst."

What I'm suggesting here is the idea of "unrisking the risk" by means of a calculated, well-designed plan. These are calculated risks.

TAKING CHARGE

When Kweisi Mfume was sixteen years old, his mother died in his arms, and he dropped out of school and worked two jobs to support his family. Finally, he got frustrated and hit the streets, where he joined a gang and just "hung out." But at twenty-two, he took charge of his life. He assumed responsibility for himself, got an education, and pursued a vision. Today, after having served nine years in the United States Congress, Mr. Mfume has just been elected president of the NAACP. His decision to go with the NAACP was a risky one. As a very popular senator, he was virtually assured of a long-term career. As president of the NAACP, he takes on an organization full of internal struggles, and if he doesn't succeed, he'll be out of a job.

If you wish to join the ranks of risk-taking self-reinventors like Kweisi Mfume, you must accept one simple principle: *Before you can take risks, you must first take responsibility*. You are in control of your own life — and no one else. Personal responsibility is the cornerstone for pursuing the risky task of self-reinvention. That's because people who don't have the courage to take responsibility for their lives won't have the courage to risk, either. How can they risk if they see their lives as already out of their control?

But assuming responsibility in no way absolves a person from a life of trials and difficulties. I have been asked, "What about when life seems to deal out bad things? Why is it that bad things always seem to happen to the same people? And why does the sun only seem to shine on the successful? Isn't life just unfair?"

Let's not kid ourselves; there are times when life is just flat unfair. I've been involved with too many tragedies to try to reduce the rationale to some silly formula. Young people contract cancer, talented people lose their jobs, devoted partners suffer through adulterous relationships.

There are as many volunteers as there are victims.

Bad things do happen. But the important thing is how you *respond* to bad things. At the risk of oversimplifying, I suggest there are two types of people when it comes to dealing with difficulties: those who assume responsibility and those who see themselves as victims.

Victims do not take risks. They see their lives as being controlled by situations and people external to themselves, therefore "totally out of their control." But as one author has gone so far as to say, "There are no such things as victims, only volunteers." It is true. Many times we volunteer into victimhood. First, we volunteer when we believe we have no control over our lives (the victim mentality) and, second, we volunteer when we fall prey to victimlike behaviors that only reinforce our helplessness.

Responsible people and victims have radically different responses to bad things. But my experience has also been that significantly fewer bad things happen to responsible people than to victims. Why is this so?

A philosophy which takes responsibility isn't thrown off course when life is difficult. When bad things happen, responsible people deal with them the best they can. A victim mentality, on the other hand, is an unempowered one. It suggests taking no action. And since "no action" is an action, the victimized person tacitly invites more difficulties. It is a regressive spiral. One with no way out — *except responsibility*.

In his best-selling book *The 7 Habits of Highly Effective People*, Stephen Covey makes a simple, yet profound, statement: "As long as you think the problem is out there, that very thought is the problem." In other words, you can be successful only when you are prepared to assume full responsibility for your own actions and attitudes. If you think the roots of your problems lie outside your sphere of influence, you have fallen prey to the victim mentality and have virtually shut off hope for growth and accomplishments because you have also shut off hope for taking necessary risks.

Matt was a pastor who messed up, big time. He made some very poor choices. Rather than face head-on his personal issues of unhappiness and discontentment, Matt chose to find relief in an extramarital affair, a choice which cost him his wife, his job, most of his friends, his self-esteem, his confidence, and his most valued possessions in the whole world — the everyday relationships with his two daughters. He became a noncustodial father.

Matt suddenly found himself out of a job, living in a small apartment rather than his roomy house, sixty miles from his home, and with only two or three people he could call friends. Because of the nature of his sin, most of his friends were baffled as to how to respond appropriately, so they chose to stay away.

At first Matt was tempted to blame himself and fall into an endless cycle of self-flagellation. Next he was tempted to blame others, in a host of ways — to blame his ex-wife for the failed marriage, to blame his friends for failing to care, to blame his colleagues for not being supportive, and to blame his spiritual professors for not teaching him well. All of that blaming would have led nowhere.

Matt, on the other hand, elected to choose "the road less traveled," the road of responsibility. He said to himself, "No matter what circumstances drove me to do what I did, I did it. It was my choice. It's now my choice to do something about it." That brave choice to take personal responsibility was Matt's first step on the arduous path of risk taking and recovery.

Stephen Covey describes two choices when dealing with adversity: One is to focus on those things within our sphere of control; the other is to focus on things outside our sphere of control. When we focus on those things within our control, we tend to make progress and accomplish our goals. But when we focus on those things beyond our sphere of control, we have a tendency to blame and complain.

It's rare to find highly successful people blaming or complaining because things haven't gone their way. Instead of blaming, they look for causes or problems that need fixing. Instead of complaining, they look for solutions. Instead of retreating, they take charge.

RISKY BUSINESS

When you assume responsibility for your life and take charge, you establish the foundation for your next necessary step: taking risks. It would be both foolish and untrue to say that your efforts of claiming a new life will be safe and guaranteed. And even if it were, it wouldn't be any fun because you love a challenge. You love defeating the wild beasts and the untamed forests, for that is how you grow. You resonate with Ranier Maria Rilke's words as quoted by David Whyte in *The Heart Aroused:* "Winning does not tempt the man. / This is how he grows: by being defeated, decisively / by constantly greater beings."

The most admired people in the world all took the risk of being defeated by the "greater beings" of fear and the need for comfort and security. Consider the risks facing one of the world's first and most famous risktakers. It begins with the words, "The LORD had said to Abram, 'Leave your country, your people and your father's household and go to the land I will show you.'... So Abram left." For Abram, who is better known as Abraham, the command to leave his own country and walk for more than one thousand miles to a strange country was a risky prospect.

As the son of a well-to-do animal herder, Abraham had acquired many possessions and a lifestyle to match. Leave his country, people, and household? Could he trust the promise of the Lord? Could he trust his own abilities? Obviously he believed he could because, as we know, the nation Israel and the whole Judeo-Christian tradition owes its roots to Abraham — a man willing to take a risk.

I find risktakers very attractive. They are willing to let go of their need for safety and move out into unmapped territories. They are brave enough to challenge their own status quo, evaluate it, keep what is good, and attempt to improve what is not, *without guarantee of success*. But not without wisdom.

THE PROBLEM WITH RISK TAKING? IT'S RISKY

What stops us from taking risks? What gets in the way of our pursuing our dreams? Fear — fear of failure, fear of embarrassment, fear of a bunch of things. But most of all, the fear that thwarts our dreams is fear of the unknown.

"Unknowns" invade that safe, critical territory we call "stability" and interrupt our rhythms, adding chaos in our already chaotic lives. "Knowns" — even bad ones — are predictable. And we are more willing to live with a bad known than any unknown. Think about the times you have chosen to live with a "bad known." Think of those who have chosen to stay in abusive relationships or those who elect to return to intolerable working conditions. We stick with bad environments because we know them; we have learned how to survive in them; we can predict the results.

In the introduction I mentioned Steve Jobs, the brilliant co-creator of Apple Computer who hounded John Sculley into coming to Apple as CEO. What I didn't tell you was "the rest of the story." After only two years at Apple, Sculley fired Jobs and had him removed from the board. So Jobs took another risk; he created NeXT Computer, which was inordinately creative but a fiscal nightmare.

Several years later, however, Jobs created yet another company,

Pixar, which designed the images for the recent Disney movie *Toy Story* — a hit that caused Pixar stock to skyrocket and made Steve Jobs a billionaire. *USA Today* said, "Steve Jobs has always had big misses and hits, and one seems to lead to the other." Jobs says of failure and risk taking: "The only time you never have a miss is if you stop trying. That's life. It's sad when people are too scared to try. Geez, I've made more mistakes than anyone I know."

For most of us, failure is devastating, especially in our success-oriented culture. In some ways, our fundamental identity is founded upon how well we succeed. We have learned to believe that each and every one of our new efforts should result in a victory, when the reality is that, like the hugely successful Steve Jobs, we all make mistakes, lots of them.

Your growth and development are directly proportionate to the level of challenge you face. In his book *Thriving on Chaos*, Tom Peters claims that the most successful companies are "into fast failures" — ones that take risk, learn, and move on. The same holds true for you. What are the risks you need to take? You probably know them well. Maybe it's learning how to work on a computer. Maybe it pertains to a relationship or a career. Whatever it is, the idea of fast failures is freeing.

It is through our mistakes and failures that we grow. Rilke's words ring out again: "This is how a man grows: by being defeated, constantly." We fear the journey into the unknown because it appears doomed to fail. However, we all know too many cases that prove just the opposite, that without risk no significant growth can ever occur. What we need to do is to create a safety net to catch us when we do fail at a new venture. Risk taking is definitely risky, but you never have to "risk everything." You just have to risk wisely.

CALCULATED RISKS

I had been in the professional ministry about two years when I concluded my first major seminar. It was a co-presentation with a man who inspired me to take many risks. Afterward he looked at me and said, "Hedges, you did really well today. In fact, I see a lot of potential. I'd love to see you attack new areas, but I fear you have some resistance. So my goal from now on is to take you out of your comfort zone, to stretch you to another level."

He was talking about risk taking, moving me from the safe to the somewhat less than safe and, by doing so, stretching me beyond my self-perceived abilities. He succeeded and was a great influence in my life. I began to understand more fully that risk does not have to be "blind." Instead, it has to be managed.

A growing field in industry today is Risk Management. Risk management always begins with "risk assessment," a careful examination of the exact nature of the risk at hand. Risk assessment is one way of making risk taking less risky. You find support for this idea in the Gospel of Luke where Jesus says, "And anyone who does not carry his cross and follow me cannot be my disciple. Suppose one of you wants to build a tower. Will he not first sit down and estimate the cost to see if he has enough money to complete it? For if he lays the foundation and is not able to finish it, everyone who sees it will ridicule him."

In this passage Jesus speaks of the risk of faith. Following him is not a matter to be taken lightly. We often speak of the "leap of faith" as if it were a blind leap into a totally unknown chasm. Not true. Indeed an aspect of the leap is blind and demands our wholly trusting God, but it is not totally blind. In essence Jesus says, "Look at me, look at my words, look at my works, look at the prophets before me, look at life as you know it, and then, if you are prepared, follow me." It is a calculated, well-thought-through decision. Risk taking involves the same process.

It's easier to look for "root blame" than "root cause."

"Calculating" your risks requires a strategy. In this strategy you articulate your objective, identify hurdles, pitfalls, and roadblocks, and create a plan to accomplish your goals. In calculating their risks, businesses widely use a planning strategy known as the PDCA: Plan, Do, Check, Act. Virtually all planning in the total quality environment uses the PDCA or some similar methodology for project planning. I believe we can use the same formula to successfully take and manage our own risks.

Before you read this final section, identify one risk you feel you need to take. Is it risking personal embarrassment? Financial failure? Family-related conflict or disapproval? Finally facing limitations of talent or ability? Keep that risk in mind and apply the principles of the PDCA to calculate your risk.

Earlier in the chapter I told you about Matt. He not only accepted responsibility, he took some major risks. At thirty-six years old, the only career Matt knew was ministry, which was no longer an option. He decided it would be best to enter the business world as a team-building consultant. Although he'd never held a position in the world of business, he did have transferable skills — speaking, strategic thinking, leadership, planning.

Nevertheless, the risk was overwhelming. He had no network, no direct experience, and waning confidence. Every time he conducted a training or intervention or facilitation, it was as if he were doing it for the first time. He hadn't developed the comfort that comes with real-life experience. Whenever he got up in front of a group of business executives, he felt he was always one question away from being thrown out the door.

Keep your own risks in mind as we see what Matt did in light of a PDCA strategy.

A PERSONAL PDCA

Plan
First Matt had to decide who he wanted to be. After doing personal assessment and talking with knowledgeable people, he saw that the field of business consulting might be a good fit. His skills matched, as did his interests and values. He even created a vision of the kind of consultant he would like to be. The beginning of any risk is the dream, the vision of something different or better, conceiving where you want to go.

Again consider your risk. Include some tangible objectives. *Exactly* where do you want to be in three months or six months? Once you determine your overall objectives, test them on other people. What kind of feedback do they offer you? Are they supportive, or do they think you've gone off the deep end?

Once Matt decided on a vision he had to assess the risk by identifying his pitfalls and hurdles. His two major business hurdles were job experience and cash flow. He was entering a new field, therefore he lacked some skills and experience. He also knew it would take some time before he could land the jobs that paid the money he needed, but since he had diligently maintained a savings account, Matt figured he could last several months on low income.

Another major risk was a blow to his ego. It's scary to enter a new field. So Matt established a strong supportive network with a couple of friends who would love him as they walked alongside in his new adventure.

After establishing his vision and understanding his risks, Matt then created a working plan. He once again evaluated his goals and then assessed his needs, his resources, his capabilities, his strengths and weaknesses, his current commitments, and a host of other things. Matt concluded that his plan must include three fundamental steps: education, affiliation, and application.

A critical element to life planning is incremental steps. Design your plan so that you're only required to take small steps at a time. Each one of these steps leads to your final goal and in an odd way provides you with a safety net in case of failure. When mountain climbers, for example, proceed up the side of a mountain, they periodically hammer a piton into the rock and secure their safety rope to the piton. If they do happen to fall, they fall only as far as the last piton. The same is true for planning. If you fail, you fall only to your last piton. The whole plan doesn't fail but only one piece of it, making it much easier to recover.

Do

Matt's plan included education, affiliation, and application. He knew he had to increase his knowledge base, so he read, attended classes, and consulted with experts in the field. He also established an affiliation with a reputable consulting firm that liked his style, recognized his potential, and was, in turn, willing to take a risk with him.

The next piece of Matt's plan was to apply his learning. This required practice. To begin with, Matt accepted every training and consulting job he could find. It didn't matter what or if it paid. His goal was to get as much experience as possible, quickly.

The failure rate for start-up businesses is as high as 80 to 90 percent. In one sense the problem can be attributed to the "doing" part of the PDCA. The problem is generally not a failure to do things right, but a failure to do the right things. You can probably guess why they failed to do the right things — they started "doing" too quickly. "Doing" is vital, but it can be a waste of time without "doing" the plan.

So what do you *do* when the plan isn't working?

Check

From a consulting group in San Francisco called Interaction Associates, I learned the definition of a great plan: A plan is a road map from which you consciously deviate. A great plan will include review sessions where you evaluate how you're doing. Are you on schedule and on budget? Are you making progress? Are you meeting your milestones? If not, what improvements or revisions do you need to make to the original plan? At these checkpoints you might even revise your overall objective.

As Matt's exposure to clients increased, it became apparent that he had created a sound vision. His clients loved his work, and he continued to get more opportunities. But when he came to the checkpoint in this process, he also discovered something he was not as good at — marketing, which his consulting firm required its consultants to do. Rather than continue to do a mediocre job in marketing, Matt created a plan by which his company might maximize the talents of delivery-oriented consultants. He took a calculated risk and presented his plan to the company's president. The company president was open to the idea and eventually changed their marketing strategy, hiring specialists who freed up people like Matt to do the work they did best.

The plan for Matt (and his consulting firm) was revisited and modified to make an even better plan.

Act

In the PDCA, this final stage occurs when you see the plan coming together (generally after several months). You not only act on your improvements and revisions, you continue to make new ones. You continue the process of planning, doing, checking, and acting until you arrive at your final destination.

Take note: Most of the time your final destination is quite different than the original plan. Frequently it is better because of all you've learned along the way. Sometimes it doesn't quite meet your lofty goals, but that too is okay because you are most likely at a much better place than where you started. You have successfully reinvented at least a part of yourself, and the process allowed for adjusting to life and to the direction of God.

Defeat can be your greatest ally.

Matt is a success story. For two years his life was a disaster. He suffered serious consequences from the poor choices he made, and he still suffers consequences today. He doesn't see his daughters every day, a few people are still angry with him, and at times he gets lonely. But there's another side, the success side. He now gets to reap the benefits of his calculated risks and responsible choices.

Today Matt loves his new church. He enjoys being just an attendee, and he loves the small Bible study group he participates in. He sees his daughters regularly, vacations with them, and shares his life with them. He has a whole new set of caring and devoted friends.

As one of the most sought-after consultants in his field, his career transition was a huge success.

So…calculated risks. By using the PDCA you can make risk taking much less risky, although not necessarily easy. Where are you with regard to risk? Are you stuck? It's understandable. I've been there. Matt has been there. Reinventing the life you want will demand that you take some risky steps, but in a calculated way. Risk is indeed risky, but it's not a throw of the dice.

There's one more way to unrisk the risk: Surround yourself with people you love. Getting the right things right will include getting the right people involved. Some of us do that very naturally. Others of us have to work at it. It's often not so easy to identify those committed and caring people we will need for support. Sometimes it takes a strategy, something like…Strategic Love.

Right Turns

RECALL THE RIGHT IDEAS

- In order to reinvent our lives, we will have to take many risks along the way.
- Risk taking doesn't have to mean we jump blindly into the unknown. It can be a well-planned endeavor, a "calculated risk."
- Before we can intentionally take risks, we must take responsibility for our lives and eradicate any "victim" mentality.

- "Calculating risks" requires a strategy that articulates our objective, identifies hurdles and pitfalls, and creates a plan to accomplish our goals.

DECIDE WHAT'S RIGHT FOR YOU

- Some people enjoy taking risks more than others. On a scale of 1–10 how would you rate your inclination to leap?
- What is the greatest risk you've ever taken? How did it pan out? Why?
- When you do risk, there's some security in stating clearly, "This is exactly what's at risk..." There's also something appealing about saying, "I want to jump without looking." Which describes your impulse better?
- Since there are no guarantees in life, how will you react if you risk and do lose something?

MAKE THE RIGHT MOVES

- Consider a risk you'd like to take and write it down. Next, list every possible outcome you can imagine, from best to worst possible and everything in between.
- Now, consider the worth of what you want to attain by your risk. Let's say you want to risk a confrontation with a friend, in hopes of clearing the air between you. How does the value of your desired end or goal stack up against the list of possible outcomes?
- It always helps to talk a risk through with a friend before taking it. Identify who could be a sounding board for your thoughts.

- If a risk looks unwise, ask yourself if there's some way to lessen the stakes or adjust the goal.

The important thing is not to think much but to love much;
and so do that which best stirs you to love.

ST. TERESA OF AVILA
FROM *THE INTERIOR CASTLE*

Jesus went up on a mountainside and called to him those he wanted, and
they came to him. He appointed twelve...that they might be with him.

MARK 3:13-14

CHAPTER NINE

STRATEGIC
LOVE

O f all the areas we would think need improvement in our lives, the last should be love. Think about it. God created us in his image, and the apostle John writes that God is love, that his very being and essence *are* love. It follows then that our essence is also love. You'd think that love would be the most natural thing we do.

In fact, there's nothing most of us fail at more regularly than loving. Even when we're at our best, we gossip about a friend's weaknesses, we secretly take joy in a colleague's failure or become indignant at his success, we frequently think more of ourselves than of our families and friends, we utter cruel and thoughtless comments, and we play one-upmanship. And when we're at our worst, we hate, we refuse to talk with a loved one turned enemy, we ensure pain, we discriminate, and we go to war.

Not a pretty picture considering our very essence is love. The tragedy is the human race has historically demonstrated how *not to love*. And it's been that way since just after the beginning, when love was corrupted and perverted — the cataclysmic effect of Adam and Eve's sin in the garden, a sin to which we still contribute daily. And from this loss of love we suffer horrible consequences — loneliness, insecurity, rejection, fear.

The greatest need in every human heart is the need for love — a real love rich with affection, support, kindness, affirmation, listening, counsel, respect, acceptance, rebuke, encouragement, touching, laughter, and shared joys, beliefs, and experiences. This rich and empowering love is also a two-way street of giving and receiving.

To love and to be loved. Everything else, including the Four Ps, is enveloped in these two: *Passion* is a matter of loving all created things; *Purpose* is directing your love inwardly in order to apply it better outwardly; *People* is the transference of love; and *Praise* is about an overwhelming love for a holy Creator.

No matter how much you have or don't have, love is one thing you can't get enough of. If you expect to live a significant reinvented life, you'll want to make sure that significant people are deeply involved and committed.

In *Habits of the Heart*, the excellent study on American social values, the authors suggest that somewhere along the line we have replaced friendship with friendliness. Our real need for heartwarming friendship is all too often sacrificed on the altar of a ubiquitous "have a nice day" superficiality.

No wonder I bristle when a bubbly waiter thinks it's his or her duty to entertain me with friendliness, a cute smile, or charming repartee. And how many of us duck when we visit churches and spot a member of the greeting committee heading our way to shake hands, find out who we are, why we're at church, and then convince us to make this family of faith our regular hangout.

I think most of us find it irritating when someone, inadvertently or not, uses "friendliness" to toy with our inherent need for intimate relationship.

I witnessed a sad event about ten years ago while attending a celebration to honor a man for twenty-five years of leadership in a major Christian organization. Part of the program was a slide show depicting the man's accomplishments and service all across the United States. The slides showed him in various cities and states, speaking, shaking hands, and being generally quite grand. Mixed in, as an attempt to commend his dedicated wife, were occasional slides of her and the kids, at home — without him. As the presentation continued, it became embarrassingly apparent that this great Christian leader was also an absentee husband and father.

At the conclusion of the slide show, it was the man's turn to do what he does best, to speak. I will never forget the moment he stepped up to the podium. He was in tears as he said, "I never really knew what a poor husband and father I have been." The event jolted me because I knew that all of us face the same temptation almost daily. Bottom line, it is the temptation to neglect the "right" things in favor of "the demand of the moment."

Careers, hobbies, recreational activities, and studies creep their way into first place in our lives. While I obviously believe those things are important, I also believe that when I am ninety and looking back, I will see a sorely mediocre life if activities have replaced people.

Of course we need people in our life. The real question is who and how many? Some of us feel overwhelmed because we have too many people who want a piece of us. Others of us wish we had too many people to choose from. Believe it or not, both suffer from the same dilemma — the inability to strategically choose who we want to be a part of our life and what part we want them to play.

STRATEGIC LOVE

Perhaps it sounds cold of me to refer to love as strategic, as if I were attempting to substitute the mysterious with the methodical. But that's not so. Love is wonderfully mysterious and filled with inexplicable surprise. But while one side of love is indeed a natural mystery, another side cannot survive and grow without feeding — like the roses in my garden. Who really knows why they bloom so artfully colored and aromatic? But when I fail to prune, water, and feed them, my roses reach only a fraction of their potential.

The same is true of loving and of being loved. Both require maintenance. You need to maintain with care both the love you give as well as the love you receive. I believe this is done best consciously, on purpose, and with a bit of a plan.

Consider these four elements of strategic love:

First: Recognize and Identify Your Need

Bill Hybels, Senior Pastor of Willow Creek Community Church, suggests that all our current relationships could be placed in one of three categories: Draining Relationships, Neutral Relationships, and Replenishing Relationships.

Draining Relationships suck the life out of you. They take what is most important to you: your energy, your joy, your emotions, and your time. Sometimes they involve people who always have a crisis you are supposed to fix; others have hidden agendas designed to change or redirect you.

The primary drawback of a draining relationship is that it is all one way; one person takes without being able to give in return. I've heard it said that draining relationships don't make friends, they take hostages. No matter how much the other person gives, it never seems to be enough.

Neutral Relationships are just that, neutral. They neither take much nor give much. Many times these are composed of your "affiliated relationships" formed around your work, church, clubs, neighbors.

Replenishing Relationships are the hardest to find. These are people you just love to be with. You track with one another; you're "in sync." You generally have similar interests and values. At the conclusion of an afternoon or evening with these folks, you feel energized, you feel heard and accepted and cared for.

Hybels suggests that we take a clean sheet of paper and create three columns. In the first column write the word "Draining;" in the second column write "Neutral;" and in the final column write "Replenishing." The chart would look like this:

Draining	Neutral	Replenishing

Place your current relationships in the appropriate columns. In some cases these relationships may be groups of people, such as coworkers or a committee you work on.

The first time I attempted Bill Hybels' exercise I was at a low place in my life where I found myself constantly drained. The results of the exercise were astounding. I discovered that, apart from my wife and one friend, all of my relationships were either draining or neutral! No wonder I was tired and frustrated.

Do you have any replenishing relationships? If so, ask yourself who they are and what replenishment they offer. If not, then your next step is to identify just what you need in a replenishing friendship. I was looking for intellectual, emotional, and spiritual camaraderie. You may need something similar, or you may need someone to share the joys and frustrations of child raising or sports or the arts or literature. Whatever it is, try to create a picture of what this person might act and feel like.

Second: "Front into Friendships"

Here is one of life's odd little truths: The older you get, the harder it is to find and make new friends.

Think back to when you were a kid. You probably had several friendships. You had your best friends and next-best friends and your next-to-the-next-best friends. When one friendship went stale, you quickly replaced it with another, with hardly a lapse of hours.

Friendships are relatively easy when you're young. Are kids just friendlier and more willing to take relational risks? Possibly. But that's not the real reason.

The real reason is opportunity. In our younger days we had tons more choices, primarily because of school. There we were surrounded by scores of kids all around the same age, with similar goals, interests, activities, and problems. Making friends was easy. In fact, we didn't really "make" many friendships at all; we "backed into" them.

But as we grow older, opportunities diminish. Maybe when you left school, you went to work for a small company. Where you once had fifty opportunities for friendships, you now have only five. Or possibly in your work environment people are more interested in getting ahead than getting close. Besides, you find that you have little in common with many coworkers, and when you do have something in common, time is too scarce to pursue a friendship.

Add to the mix that you are now more reserved and a little more cautious regarding relationships than you were as a kid. You have developed a fear of rejection. Backing into friendships becomes less and less frequent. As a result, you find yourself with precious few, if any, replenishing relationships. So, what do you do?

I suggest that rather than passively waiting to back into a friendship, you aggressively "front into friendships." This is a calculated, yes even strategic, approach. Fronting into friendships is recognizing your need, identifying an opportunity, and then pursuing it with wisdom and grace.

I was thirty-eight when I took Bill Hybels' relationship quiz and discovered I had few replenishing relationships. I knew I had to do something. I evaluated my list of neutral relationships to see if I could nurture any of those into replenishing ones. Those options were not good. My only real choice was to "make a new friend." How depressing. I had no idea how to begin. But I began to ponder.

I thought of one guy who lived in the same area as I did. We had met, lunched, and chatted a few times. He seemed like my kind of guy — a thinker, kind of cynical, a little bit of a revolutionary, and also deeply passionate about his life and his friends. When we were together, we seemed to click. So I increased the frequency of our lunch meetings, and soon it became apparent to me that Terry could indeed be a replenishing friend.

My next step was the most difficult. I told him about the evaluating I'd been doing and that I needed more good friends. I explained the kind of friend I was looking for. Yes, it felt a bit awkward. And yet it was necessary because replenishing friendships require commitment, honesty, and clear expectations.

To my relief and delight Terry responded with four words: "Let's go for it." As with all things in life, we had no guarantees, just a promise to give it a real shot. Eight years later Terry remains one of the best friends I've ever had. We truly click. At certain times he's understood me like no other. Our friendship is a gift, but one that came by asking, not by accident.

I now have a handful of replenishing relationships, and among that handful are three main men, guys who know me inside and out, and each offers me a different perspective and a different kind of friendship. Of these three guys, two of them were "fronted into."

You choose your friends at some risk, but you let them choose you at your own.

How about you? If you have identified a need for replenishing relationships, you may begin to see old friends and acquaintances through a different filter. You may possibly discover a close friend in someone you have known for a long time but haven't taken the time to pursue. Or maybe you will have to keep your eyes wide open. When you find a potential friendship, advance slowly, gracefully, and with patience. If after knowing a person for only a week, you approach him or her with the idea of pursuing a committed friendship, you will likely chase him or her away.

Instead, find a way to hang out together. Bring up important subjects of conversation to see how well you really do click. If after several weeks or months you still think this friendship has great possibilities, then go full steam ahead. You may wish to discuss the direction of the friendship — what you each expect and need from it. As awkward as it may feel, clarity can be relational salvation. I have seen more relationships dissolve and turn to anger simply because each person had a different expectation of the other and of the relationship.

Third: Fill the Vacuum

A good marriage is probably the most replenishing of all relationships. No one has the opportunity to know you better than a spouse. You eat together, sleep together, and share the same responsibilities, concerns, and joys. In marriage the opportunities for true connection are vast, but the unfortunate reality is that far too many marriages are more neutral (or even draining) than they are replenishing.

Still, the depth of your ability to replenish one another is a matter of choice. Just as you chose to commit to one another on your wedding day, in the same way you can choose to commit to a deep friendship within your marriage. My point here is not to fix broken marriages but to encourage those who are simply neglecting their spousal commitments of love and nurture.

Marriage, friendship, and love require attention. They all wilt without it. And I believe attention to a loved one must be given *intentionally*, on purpose. I came upon a journal entry of a guy writing to his wife. He gave me permission to print it. Note the critical dimension of intentionality.

We had a fight today. It's odd I would use the word "fight."
They're not fights really. Our words are like clumps of air formed
in the gut and expelled into the vacuum that happens to be

floating between us, are created by insufficient attention; and it's the fighting words that fill this vacuum because as we all know, nature abhors a vacuum. But the fighting words are not all that bad; they're necessary, and while they have potential for harm, they're harmless because what they really are is shocking.

So it's the fighting words that shock us into the realization that we have a vacuum — this sort of temporary nothingness hanging between us — demanding to be filled, and we find ourselves with two choices: fill it with love or fill it with anger. And we always opt for the former. We love. Because that's what we do and when we don't, we use the fighting words as shock therapy. Just to remind us how much we each need to care for the other.

You might think of your significant relationships as an empty container, one that can be filled with either love or not love. Committed relationships cannot stay neutral. They don't have that sort of luxury. When you fail to fill the container with loving things like support, affirmation, trust, and respect, nature will fill it for you with destructive things like doubt, fear, and criticism.

Filling the vacuum is a choice you must make if you wish to maintain any replenishing relationship, whether it be in your marriage or in your vital friendships. It is another aspect of being strategic about love.

Fourth: "Manage" the Relationship

As already pointed out, replenishing relationships do not grow by accident; they require care. Two foremost issues would be quantity and quality. How frequently do you contact those you consider to be replenishing relationships? When you meet, is there any kind of plan or agenda? What kinds of things are needed in each relationship? These questions are good ones to consider.

I know guys who have weekly breakfast meetings or regular tennis times or monthly gatherings where their families get together. With two of my friends I have committed to interacting no less than two times every month; with the third, who travels as much as I do, we try to touch base one time per month. But we give ourselves permission not to be rigid. Sometimes my contact with these guys is several times per week, other times much less frequent. However, in the long run I know that without regular, committed contact these relationships will suffer.

Frequency is not the only thing you manage. You also manage the quality of the relationships. A good start is to determine the needs of your most important and replenishing relationships. Children require devoted time for talking, reading, playing, and observing. Spouses require lots of talk and touch times. And friends expect a host of different things, depending on the friend and the time. And then of course you will have to decide how to do what. Some families commit to eating the evening meal as a family. "Date night" is a popular option for many marriages. I have an agreement with a friend who lives in another state to write one letter per month.

The real reason you need to manage your replenishing relationships is that you have far too many demands on your time and energies. One of the greatest rewards of managing your friendships according to "strategic love" is the freedom it gives you to say yes to good relationships, and no to draining and neutral ones. And when you say no, you're not doing it because these are not good people; you're doing it because significant living demands using your time most wisely.

Some friendships may happen by accident, but they survive on purpose.

The question has been asked of me in the past, "How do I say no to someone who needs me? I don't want to be rude, and I am certainly reluctant to inflict any pain."

It is a decent concern, but when I hear this question, my first thought is to wonder about the true motivation. I may ask in return, "What are you really concerned about, their feelings or your image?" It's a hard question, and I probably sound pretty callous. However, remember the third of the Wrong Rules: "the need to be needed." You have a limited amount of time in a day, and you must use it wisely. Believe it or not, you're not called to be a messiah in anyone's life, a job description which, by the way, has already been filled by inordinately high quality staff.

Look at your normal day as a bucket. At the end of every day that bucket will be filled with rocks. To fill your bucket, you have a virtual geological museum from which to make your selections. There are all kinds of rocks: work rocks, friend rocks, play rocks, food rocks, phone rocks, and meeting rocks. You have the choice to fill it with the rocks you want…or you can hang around waiting for needy and draining rocks to jump in — and they will.

Consider that replenishing people "need" you just as much as draining people — maybe even more. Time for your significant and replenishing relationships *must* be your "rock of choice." Give yourself permission to throw them into your bucket first because they will take care of you as you take care of them. It will mean saying no to some people. But then, ironically, you will be strengthened to serve the people who truly need you (the draining people). And when you serve them with a storehouse of personal strength, you may find that they are no longer quite as draining.

I'm not advocating a form of egocentricity where you think only of yourself. In fact I am suggesting quite the opposite. As you will read in chapter twelve, I believe you will be most fulfilled when you serve others. However, you will serve them much more effectively when you know how to reconcile your own vital relational needs.

Jesus knew his years of earthly ministry were limited. His plan was secure and immutable. He also knew that, given the chance, every person he touched would want as much of his time as he was willing to give. But he was cautious, at times wisely deferring instead of serving. The Scripture says that sometimes Jesus chose to leave a place even when people were demanding his time.

He even chose to limit his closest relationships to twelve, and of the twelve he selected three to be his "inner circle." So the question is this: If God on earth knew that he had to limit the scope of his relationships, why do we think we can do more?

WHAT NEXT?

So far in the book we have articulated many of the right things you'll want to get right. There's the power of the Four Ps and passionate living. You know the value of rejecting the wrong rules in favor of the ones you were created to follow, and you have a system to follow your dreams. You know about developing a rich interior life in order to create the stability necessary to make the required changes, and you've discovered that risk doesn't necessarily have to be so risky. In this chapter the unparalleled value of relationships has once again been supported.

In the final section of the book we look at "making moves that count." In essence, how you can take all you have learned and put it to use so that in the end you will say, "My life has truly mattered."

Right Turns

RECALL THE RIGHT IDEAS

- Love isn't easy, even in the best of circumstances. Even though we were created to love, we are naturally not as loving as we could be.
- In order to reinvent fulfilling lives, we must be strategic in our approach to love and relationships.
- Right relationships rarely happen automatically — and if we let them, draining relationships, which don't help *anyone* in

the long run, can consume all our relationship time.

- As we attempt to love strategically, it *is* possible to be sacrificial as well as self-caring.

DECIDE WHAT'S RIGHT FOR YOU

- What qualities do you most desire in a friendship?
- Who, if anyone, do you feel close to and trust right now? Why?
- What qualities do you most desire in a spouse or very best friend?
- Which of these areas seem most promising: people at work, people you knew in the past but have lost touch with, someone who shares the same hobbies or interests, or friends of friends?

MAKE THE RIGHT MOVES

How to "front into friendship":

- Keep it casual.
- Start with a short time frame for the first get-together.
- Have an activity to focus on, even if it's eating.
- Listen carefully, and take some risks to express yourself as well.
- Don't be *only* the "pursuer," and by the same token, don't wait to be "pursued."
- Set a specific time, if possible, for the next get-together. "I'll call you" is too vague.
- Still no luck? Go for more radical strategies. Change seats at church, start a reading group, volunteer one day a month, or take a class that interests you. Add two ideas to this list.

PART FOUR

Carving Your Mark Deep

Making moves that matter

Your thinking is right, you know your assets, and you've begun to make some strategic moves. You are on the road to reinventing the life you really want. But will your life make a difference in the people and places that count? In this section you will understand the keys to carving your mark deep, and in the right places.

Every Hun has value — even if only to serve as a bad example.

WES ROBERTS
FROM *LEADERSHIP SECRETS*
OF ATTILA THE HUN

If…you pay special attention to the [man] who is wearing the fine
clothes…and you say to the poor man,…"Sit down by my footstool,"
have you not made distinctions among yourselves, and
become judges with evil motives?

JAMES 2:3-4, NASB

CHAPTER TEN

EXTREME
DIGNITY

I f you got all the "right things right" and were a successfully reinvented person, would anyone else care?

What difference would it make to someone you've merely encountered, like a salesclerk? Would that person observe something different about you, something uncommon and yet desirable?

Imagine you were in the business of self-reinvention and that you were required to have a marketing strategy to promote yourself. One vital component would be your public-relations policy, which is the art of influencing how the public perceives you. I want to suggest one behavior that will make you "gold" in the eyes of the people around you (your "public") while at the same time align you with the truest thing in your heart. This is another of those "really right things." It's called extreme dignity.

According to a recent study, 70 percent of workers are dissatisfied with the way their bosses manage them. In response to a plethora of complaints, the study cited three primary things workers wanted from their management: to receive clear direction, to be treated with respect, and to have input into decisions that affect them. Clear expectations, respect, and input. In essence, workers want to be treated as inherently valuable, as deserving dignity.

Joan Posluzny is a high-level manager in a large corporation. She's a strong manager who knows exactly what she wants and has a reputation for getting results. But Joan has another reputation as well. She listens attentively to the wild ideas of her colleagues and ponders the suggestions of the people who report to her. As a result, her employees and consultants would follow her anywhere. It has a lot to do with the way Joan treats people. She acts as if every person is intrinsically valuable, so she regularly gives them dignity.

We all long for the Joan Posluznys of the world who will treat us the way we feel we deserve. Instead, what we often get are the people who tell us our work is not good enough, fast enough, or new enough; or that we don't talk right, dress right, eat right, or look right.

Every human being longs for dignity. As a successfully reinvented person, you will never carve a deeper mark than the mark you carve on the hearts of people dying to be dignified. And, in return, you will never feel more significant than when you embark upon the road to extreme dignity. I call it extreme dignity not because it is radical (although it is), but because it is so uncommon. It's one thing we want, and, unfortunately, one thing we rarely find.

ROYAL TREATMENT

Why do people naturally feel they deserve dignity? The answer is found in the first chapter of the Bible: "So God created man in his own image, in the image of God he created him; male and female he created them." The desire for dignity is an inherent human trait.

In a novel by C. S. Lewis entitled *Perelandra*, we encounter a hero named Ransom, who suddenly finds himself transported from Earth to a pristine planet called Perelandra. The planet is perfect and untainted by sin, just the way God intended it to be from the beginning. The most powerful scene in the book comes at the end when Ransom finally sees the man and the woman (the Adam and Eve figures) together after having defeated the tempter. The sight of them is so majestic that he falls uncontrollably on his face in worship.

Ransom fell on his face in worship because when he looked upon the man and the woman, it was as if he were looking upon God. The man and the woman, without the tarnish of sin, looked so much like God himself that Ransom *couldn't tell the difference.*

We take too lightly the scripture that tells us about creation. Man and woman were formed in God's very image, an incredible and almost incomprehensible concept. Ransom caught it. And if we did, we'd treat other people a lot differently than we do.

PRACTICAL DIGNITY

Extreme dignity is a very practical idea. It rarely calls for going out of your way, and it takes up no more of your time. It only calls for a consideration of your extreme value and the value of the people around you. It applies to everyone you encounter — family, friends, acquaintances, colleagues, coworkers, neighbors, clients, waiters, salesclerks, and airline attendants.

The art of dignifying is an engaging, two-way street of giving and receiving. One of the beauties of offering dignity to others is that it has a way of coming back around to benefit the giver. You too need dignity. It is vital to your self-reinvention. But like many of life's backward principles, the best way to get it is by giving it.

---

*The more you feel the need for dignity the more
you need to give some away.*

The person who makes a habit of giving dignity to others creates a royal environment around himself. Other people just naturally feel good in his presence and respond in kind. Offering dignity can open new doors, recover lost opportunities, make an immediate impression of love, and cause your life to be remembered in the small ways that count. Plus, you never know when you will want the same respect back. The waiter you honor today may own the restaurant tomorrow and be hiring your daughter next year.

If extreme dignity is also practical dignity, then what are some of the "practical" behaviors for offering dignity? To keep it simple I'd say it's all about how you listen, what you say, and what you do.

Listen Soulfully

When I was a pastor, one of my key job responsibilities was small-group ministries. I created programs, trained facilitators, wrote curriculum, and managed the department. I based the premise for developing people and programs on three primary relational needs: We all have the need to be heard, the need to be accepted, and the need to be cared for.

It's the need to be heard that's often the hardest to meet. In a stirring scene from the first *Crocodile Dundee* movie, Croc and Linda are standing on a balcony outside a New York hotel. Linda is trying to explain to Croc why she has to leave for a couple of hours. The conversation goes something like this:

Linda: *Sorry Crocodile, I have to leave for a couple of hours.*
  I'm going to see my therapist.
Croc: *Oh, what's a therapist?*
Linda: *He's someone I talk to once a week for about an hour.*
Croc: *What do you talk about?*
Linda: *I tell him how things have gone during the week, about*
  my joys and fears and frustrations and accomplishments.
  I pretty much just tell him how I'm feeling.
At this point Crocodile Dundee has a very puzzled look on his
  face as if he can't quite catch what she's saying.

Linda notices and says, "Well, all my friends also go to therapists."

To which Croc responds so brilliantly in his strong Australian accent, "Don't they have any mates?"

I love it. As much as I believe in the usefulness of psychotherapy, I have to agree with Croc that there would be fewer therapists today if people had more "mates" or friends who would simply listen to what they had to say. Studies show that in a normal conversation, the person listening will truly hear only 20 to 30 percent of what you say. Imagine, 70 to 80 percent of your words just float out into the air!

What if you were the one to break that horrible cycle of non-listening? What if you were the one who devoted just a little more energy to hearing the words of the people around you? The subtle, yet powerful, impact would be astounding. Let me offer a couple of suggestions on how to begin.

I cover several principles and techniques in the listening modules I teach corporations. The techniques include using good non-verbals, repeating and paraphrasing what you have heard, and generally showing that you are interested. But of all the techniques, a couple of simple ones can make the greatest impact.

Resist your first temptation to talk. Remember, people are dying to be heard, and they can't be heard when you're talking. I am not suggesting that you say nothing. In fact, it's good for you to respond. Just resist *your first temptation.* Resisting your first temptation allows the other person just a little more time.

Resist the temptation to talk about yourself. It's amazing, but we have the tendency to turn every conversation into one about ourselves. It happens almost every time. And when it does, it devalues the person speaking.

A common saying is, "People don't care how much you know till they know how much you care." While trite, it's true. And I can think of no better way to show you care than by attentive listening.

Talk Wisely

A man we'll call Frank got into a terrible mess — the kind of mess that cost him his job and even some friendships. It also cost him his stellar reputation because as people discovered his trouble, some began to tell others about it. And those people in turn told others, who told others, and on it went. In a short time, what should have been a closely held, private matter was now widely known throughout the community.

A few months later one of the gossipers came to Frank to apologize and ask forgiveness — a commendable behavior. Frank, being the quality person he is, accepted the apology and forgave the man his error. But when the man asked if he could do anything to remedy his error, Frank told him the story of the goose.

In order to remedy his error, Frank explained, the man would have to catch a goose, pluck all its feathers, and put them in a bag. He was then to take the bag of feathers to the top of a church steeple and empty the bag into the wind so that the feathers blew all over the town. The final step was to wait one day, then go out and collect each and every feather and put it back onto the goose. "That," said Frank to the gossiper, "is the chance you have of ever repairing the reputation you have tarnished with your unguarded tongue."

One of the greatest, most frequent, and least acknowledged sins in the church concerns the way we talk. The New Testament letters are replete with comments about the good use of words as well as the harmful.

Uncarefully spoken words can be killers. In a very real sense, we recreate people with words. Let me explain. I had a friend we'll call Bill. Bill went to seminary with John, whom I was just getting to know. When Bill discovered that I was considering John for a backup speaker, he told me I had better stay away from John because of his questionable character.

Having this negative picture of John, for a long time I was reluctant to befriend him. But as time went on and I got to know him better, I discovered that John was a great guy who had been misrepresented to me. Bill had created a false reality in my mind.

Your words will destroy or dignify the people who surround you. The following is a brief list of ways you can dignify people with words.

1. Regularly affirm those around you. If a colleague did a good job, tell him. When your wife looks especially great, tell her. Anytime you notice something special or particularly noteworthy about a person, say so.

2. Refuse to gossip, and refuse to listen to gossip. Keep in mind that whatever "gossip-worthy" information you have about a person

is at best only half-true. If someone appears to be gossiping, an easy response is "Why are you telling me this?" When word gets out that you will not listen to such talk, two things will happen: People will be reticent to tell you gossip, and others will be eager to tell you of important personal matters because they will feel they have found someone to trust.

3. Be very careful about "naming" people — "Greg is so lazy;" "Sandi never does her work right" — because when you do, you have colored the way others view that person.

4. Keep your word. If you tell someone you will do something, then do it.

Act Empoweringly

"Empowerment" is one of the watchwords in business today. And as watchwords go, it has become trite and overused. Nevertheless, it's a great concept. To act empoweringly encourages others to take responsibility as you honor their actions and ideas. The person dedicated to empowering others has discovered yet another way of expressing extreme dignity.

Phil Cavanaugh is a federal relations manager for a multinational energy company. In 1995 I facilitated an Upward Feedback Session with him and his direct reports. (Upward feedback is a process by which employees are given the opportunity to evaluate the performance of their boss.)

As Phil's direct reports listed his strengths, I was struck by his ability to relate to people at all levels of the company. It was said that

Phil could go out into the field in the morning, put on work boots and a hard hat and chat with employees, then later that same evening have dinner with a United States senator. And each person would feel that Phil was on track with him. He listens carefully to whoever is speaking to him. And he doesn't talk down to anyone.

Jim Muller was the manager of staff and field personnel in a large Canadian oil field. I have met no man more loved and fewer men more dedicated to achieving lofty targets. Although Jim frequently had ideas and strategies about how to reach company targets, he also had a knack for empowering people to make their own decisions and create their own plans. He knew this was the route to success, both company success and the success of his people. Jim acted in ways that empowered and accomplished results.

Do people like Jim and Phil just have a knack for this stuff, or is it a conscious effort? I believe it is a conscious choice to recognize the inherent value of every person. "Acting empoweringly" is about the things you can do to bestow dignity. Here are just a few ideas.

1. Accept others' failures as their steppingstones to success. One of the greatest compliments a leader can receive is that he or she led people to success along a growing path of learning experiences.

2. Encourage and assist others to "do it themselves." Many people lack confidence in their ability until they discover someone who believes in them.

3. Give credence to ideas, beliefs, and opinions different from your own. We would do well to remember that we are only human and that we too can be wrong. I don't suggest always agreeing with

opinions that are different than yours, just giving the other person the dignity to think and believe what he will.

4. Return phone calls promptly. It may sound silly, but nothing makes me feel less valued than when someone doesn't return a phone call. And on the other hand, "dignifiers" who regularly return calls promptly are extremely rare.

5. At public gatherings seek out people who are standing alone. We all know there is no lonelier place than in a crowd. An extreme dignifier will seek out those people if only to say, "Hi."

When I was on staff at the church one of my favorite colleagues was Jack Lesch, the church custodian. I loved Jack. He was a "real guy." Jack and I spent a lot of time together planning and organizing, but we also goofed around a lot and had a great time.

As chief custodian, Jack was responsible for more than one hundred thousand square feet of office and auditorium space. A mistake made by too many people was to view Jack as the custodian instead of the minister of moving stuff and keeping the joint going. I can't tell you the number of jams Jack pulled me out of, largely due to our friendship. Jack's retirement was the only roast I have ever truly enjoyed giving. He was almost impossible to replace.

A sad tendency we all have is to undervalue people because of position, education, or affiliation. Doing so robs those persons of the dignity they need. Every human being has a gaping hole in his heart that longs to be treated royally. It is our birthright. We're born in the highest image in all the cosmos, the image of God. We all deserve to be listened to, to be spoken of with honor, and to be treated with utmost respect.

WHAT TO DO WHEN YOU DON'T WANT TO

It's easy enough to give dignity to people who are nice to us or to those who are "needier" than us, but what about giving dignity to cranky, ornery, mean people — the guy who "just doesn't like you," or the insensitive, dominating person on your work team, or the "holier than thou" deacon, or the next-door neighbor with the barking dogs? You know who I mean. How does a reinvented person dignify these folks?

It ain't easy. But someone's gotta do it. Let me give you two principles.

First is the *Empathy Principle*. The Empathy Principle suggests that when you consider that difficult individual, you don't see a "difficult person," but rather a "difficult behavior." This is a critical distinction because it depersonalizes the conflict. It allows you to analyze the roots of the issue more clearly.

For example, when you consider Rob — the insensitive, domineering man in your work group — your normal response is to say that Rob is just a jerk (and he might be). But when you use the Empathy Principle, you ask yourself why Rob is so insensitive and dominating. Maybe he's insecure; maybe no one ever really listens to him; maybe he has heard the office gossip about him; and maybe no one has treated him kindly and as an equal.

When you consider those factors, Rob elicits more respect and human dignity. Keep in mind, though, the *Empathy Principle* is rarely our first response to a difficult behavior. Generally, our first response is to get rankled and frustrated and pretty much want to smack the culprit. But wisdom can prevail with the help of empathy. It takes work, and it takes time, and it is powerful.

The second principle is related but strikes closer to home. It is the *I Am Them Principle*. At any given time you and I *are* those cranky, ornery, mean people. We all are frequently insensitive, dominating, self-centered, and a general nuisance to others. It's part of being human. And the greater our ability to tap into our humanness — our pain and subsequent "difficult behaviors" — the greater our ability to empathize with the needs in others. It's the secret to recognizing the inherent worth of every human being.

Those most ashamed deserve the most dignity.

Extreme dignity is one of those "really right things" to get right. Although it has a lot to do with how you treat others, it is also about how you view yourself. We're talking about Jesus' "golden rule" — treating others just as you wish to be treated. Acknowledging your own "royal" value is the beginning to responding to it in others. As the reinvented person comes ever closer to the person he or she wants to be, extreme dignity will be one of the greatest assets and pleasures.

Right Turns

RECALL THE RIGHT IDEAS

- Because we are created in God's image, every human being has an inherent need to be treated with dignity.
- We will never carve a mark deeper than the one we carve when we grant dignity, especially to someone who has given up on receiving it.
- Extreme dignity is also practical dignity. Three basic ways we can give it are to listen soulfully, speak wisely, and act empoweringly; it's about how you listen, what you say, and what you do.
- When granting dignity is hard to do, the *Empathy Principle* and the *I Am Them Principle* can help us get the right perspective.

DECIDE WHAT'S RIGHT FOR YOU

- What is the difference between someone who *carries* himself with dignity and someone who bestows it?
- Give examples in society of people not being treated with dignity.
- In what tangible ways have people given you dignity when you most needed it — for example, during a divorce or a crisis in your career?
- Are there people you find it hard to offer dignity — because they don't behave in a way that seems dignified? How do the *Empathy* and *I Am Them Principles* apply?

MAKE THE RIGHT MOVES

- One way to grant people dignity is to assume the best and appeal to a person's highest self in spite of any evidence to the contrary. Think of two tangible ways you might grant this kind of dignity this week.

- To bestow dignity is to ascribe to someone his *right* value — the incomprehensible, unconditional love that God offers. How, specifically, might you communicate this kind of dignity to someone today?

- List ten specific ways that you might communicate dignity to strangers and acquaintances such as bank tellers, or the crabby cashier at the midnight market. Note the person's response when you bestow dignity.

Imagine two children playing hide-and-seek; one hides but
the other does not look for him. God is hiding and man is not seeking.
Imagine His distress.

ELIE WIESEL
FROM *SOULS ON FIRE*

"Your name will no longer be Jacob, but Israel, because
you have struggled with God."

GENESIS 32:28

CHAPTER ELEVEN

THE GOD FIGHTERS

How can I write a chapter about God when the one thing I have learned after years of studying theology is that to know anything at all about God is to understand that I know next to nothing about him? And how can I suggest to you that the significance of your reinvented life will be directly proportionate to the size of your God, when I refuse to prescribe a formula for understanding a God who will not allow himself to be defined by a formula?

And yet, how can I not suggest exactly this because the most significant reinvented life will be intimately connected to a great and huge God. Just as you were built with an innate need to accomplish good things and an innate need to love, you were also created with an innate need to worship. This truth is yet another of those very right things to get right. It's the one thing that offers hope, meaning, and destiny. We're talking about the final of the Four Ps — passion, purpose, people, and *praise*.

We've talked a lot about strategies, risk, and change — all requiring action, and all very important for reinventing our lives. But *believing* the right things is just as crucial as *doing* them. In fact, we can't do the right things if we don't *believe* the right things. What we perceive to be true about God will affect every area of the life we are trying to form. As it turns out, the bigger our God, the bigger our life.

However, we're faced with another of life's great paradoxes: The very thing we were created to do — to love and praise this great God — is surely one of life's greatest challenges. We've been told a lot of things, we believe a lot of things, but somehow, when it comes to worship, we frequently still find it hard to get it right.

If I were to ask you to create a list of activities you could do to praise God and to develop a richer "spiritual side," you could come up with a list of commendable ideas, including prayer, Scripture reading, attending church, taking communion, volunteer service, and Bible studies. All of these are vital activities for the person seeking connection with God and the Christian community.

In fact, you already know these, so maybe we should just "close in prayer" and move on to the final chapter.

Then again, just because we know these things doesn't mean we've developed the kind of relationship with God that we want. Most of us recognize a chasm between the way we'd like to relate to God (or worse, the way we feel we "ought to relate") and the way we currently do. And because we have an intuitive sense of the kinds of activities that would be helpful, we often start out on the right track only to get derailed. An understanding of what causes those derailments might be a logical starting point for reinventing our beliefs.

THE SHRINK-WRAPPED GOD

Perhaps you're familiar with the Christian classic *Your God Is Too Small*, a well-conceived book about enlarging one's beliefs about God. Well, I would like to add that it's possible our God is also too safe, too agreeable, too impassionate, and too understandable. Of course, God isn't *really* these things, but sometimes in our effort to get Him within our grasp, we reinvent Him in our own minds, rather than being reinvented by His.

Is your God...

Too Safe?

It's terrible to be misunderstood. Imagine what it would be like for Jesus. Is there anyone in history about whom people have had a wider variety of opinions? A common perception of Jesus is that he's caring and emotive, soft and cuddly, always accepting, rarely judging, never angry (except with the *bad guys*). One big bundle of love. Kind of like a big Leo Buscaglia in the sky. But there is far more to Jesus than this image of a Buscaglian teddy bear.

In the classic allegory *The Chronicles of Narnia*, C. S. Lewis takes his readers on a journey with four children to an enchanting land called Narnia. In the following dialogue, the four young heroes have just entered Narnia for the first time, where they discover the entire land is in danger of being destroyed by the evil Queen. While visiting the Beavers, our heroes learn that help is on the way and that his name is Aslan, the great lion.

> "Is — is he a man?" asked Lucy.
>
> "Aslan a man?" said Mr. Beaver sternly. "Certainly not. I tell you he is King of the Wood and the son of the great Emperor-Beyond-the-Sea. Don't you know who is King of the Beasts? Aslan is a lion — the Lion, the great Lion."
>
> "Oh?" said Susan. "I'd thought he was a man. Is he — quite safe?"
>
> "Safe?" said Mr. Beaver. "...Who said anything about safe? 'Course he isn't safe. But he's good."

Not safe, but good. Believe it or not, that is the New Testament Jesus. At Christian seminars I love to ask the question, "If Jesus, clothed in all his divine and kingly regalia, were to walk into this room right this minute, what would you do?" The responses vary. Some say, "I'd run to him, greet him, and praise him." Others say their hearts would melt with joy. Others would bow in worship.

But my guess is, if Jesus were to walk into the room, arrayed in all his divine radiance, you would fall on your face in absolute terror. That's what happened when John, the disciple whom Jesus loved, saw Jesus in his fully divine state on the island of Patmos. In Revelation 1, John says, "I fell at his feet like a dead man."

Just as C. S. Lewis hinted, Jesus is not safe — he is a holy God in the midst of an unholy people. Jesus is not safe — the demons (thousands of times more powerful than humans) tremble at the sound of his name. Jesus is not safe — every knee will one day bow to him. Not because it's the fashionable thing to do, but because it's the *only* thing to do. Every created thing will realize it has come face to face with its Maker, with God.

To think you understand God fully is to misunderstand him altogether.

Jesus, the God who loves you, who died for you, who even serves you, is no wimpy, limp-wristed God. He is a being more powerful and more terrifying than anything you can imagine. Is he safe? No way. But he's good!

Too Agreeable?

Whenever I listen to Christian radio and hear the speaker begin a sentence with the phrase "God wants...," I know I'm probably in for an interesting account of God and Scripture. That's because his next words are generally something like, "God wants you to be happy" or "...to be fulfilled" or "...to be emotionally healthy" or "...to be prosperous." Those are quite different from Jesus' words when he declares that I'm blessed when I'm poor, hungry, hated, and ostracized.

In my mind the popular praise song "He Is Able" addresses the wrong question. I don't think anyone who believes in God ever asks if he is able, but rather if he is willing. And it is a much more appropriate question since no one knows the mind of God.

I'm afraid the "Agreeable God Syndrome" has led many to the notion that one of God's big purposes is to answer prayer, kind of like Aladdin's genie. The irony is that we really don't *want* a God who agrees with our conclusions and our requests.

My three-year-old son is "all boy," and if left to his own devices, he would be even more "all boy" — more than any of us could take. While he may not like me to tell him no, it gives him security in his inner being. He utterly depends upon the disciplined structure his parents lay out for him.

It is the same with us adults. We don't crave a God who waits around for us to tell him what to do. We want a God with chutzpah. One who knows how to take charge and does so. Like the not-so-safe God, we want a God who knows he's God. Sometimes he says yes, sometimes he says no. But most times he just waits patiently for us to figure it out on our own, while he gently guides in ways we can't always understand. Usually after a time of reflection, we look back and see his hand all along the way.

Too Impassionate?

One of my favorite Bible stories is about the renaming of Jacob because it is actually quite a strange story. Jacob, on the eve of a potentially life-threatening rendezvous with his brother, has an encounter with God himself in which he spends an entire night "wrestling with God." When the morning comes, Jacob refuses to let go until God blesses him. As a result, God names him "Israel," which means "one who fights or contends with God."

Imagine, an entire nation of followers to be called "God Fighters." I think that says something about God. He is not a flat, one-dimensional being who expects his people to respond robotically. It's as if he is encouraging us to approach him passionately. Relationship with God is something worth fighting for. Just like in the medieval novels where the damsels are overcome with love for the knights who fight dragons to get to them, in the same way our God is overcome with love when his people fight to love him. Even if it calls for fighting God himself.

I picture us like Jacob, as we hold onto his leg and scream, "No way. I won't let you go. No matter what, I won't let you go until we are fully intimate."

God is not distant or aloof or hanging out in heaven just watching the show. He is passionately involved, and Scripture encourages you and me to be the same way. We access God most fully when we get in touch with the fullness of our humanity — our needs, fears, loves, and questions. Ron Bauer, Reverend of St. Margaret's Episcopal Church, says, "The first Adam tried to be God and was an utter failure, while the second Adam (Christ) tried to be fully human and saved the world."

Too Understandable?

Systematic theology is a very useful discipline. It packages Scripture in such a way that we can more fully understand the wonder, purpose, and plan of God. But there is also an inherent danger in "systematic theology." The danger is that while theology may be "systematic," God doesn't always seem to be. More often he is mysterious, confounding, and downright opposite. Just when you think you've got his number, he changes it.

In the New Testament we find John the Baptist in jail for being more prophetic than King Herod could handle. Only months earlier John had proclaimed to the world that Jesus was the Christ, but during his stay in prison he began to question Jesus. Jesus was behaving in ways that didn't fit John's "theology." So, in Matthew's gospel we are told that John sent word to ask Jesus, "Are you the one we've been expecting?"

Jesus' response was for all of us to hear. "Blessed is he who does not stumble over me." In other words, "Let me be God. Watch and learn. Don't let your theology get in the way."

Sometimes I wonder if we haven't "shrink-wrapped" God so tightly in our minds that even *he* has a hard time breaking out. However, he refuses to be confined to any tightly construed theology. Humans need theology; it helps us understand God. We need systems; they offer clarity. But we have to remember that God is the God of the system too. And no matter what we believe about God, he is more.

NOT THE EXPECTED WAY

When John the Baptist sent word to ask whether Jesus was the "expected one," Jesus' response was, in essence, "Yes, I am the expected one. It's just that I haven't come the expected way." John expected Jesus to establish a literal kingdom among the people, while Jesus came to establish a kingdom in people's hearts.

Every now and then each of us needs our own spiritual revolution in which the Christ once again proves himself to be the expected one, but not in the expected way. The unexpectedness of God keeps our relationship fresh and vital. It rekindles the heart, and then our lives bear out the truth of what a great God we have.

As you've considered reinventing your life, how has God figured in? You run the risk of having a small life if you have a small God. So if you have fallen prey to a view of a shrink-wrapped God (and we all do), how can you go about breaking open the wrapping so God can burst out?

Jesus is certainly the "expected one" in our lives, but rarely does he come in the "expected way."

It doesn't require you to abandon anything you currently believe about God. Actually, it's just the opposite. My goal is for all of us to add to what we currently believe, to expand our vision of God, and to allow Him to reveal Himself in ways that are ever-increasing in magnificence.

Tom Thompson is an ACF — Adult Child of a Fundamentalist. Raised in a tradition with profound reverence for and obedience to God, Tom had the gospel planted deeply in his soul. For him God was as real as life itself. But as Tom entered his thirties and forties, he found that something was amiss in his soul. His God had become, for him, too shrink-wrapped and therefore so had his own life.

So Tom set about reinventing his life with God. After long and numerous discussions with Tom and others like him, I have found four hallmarks of those people who allow God to break out of the tight little box and really show himself.

One: They Explore the Land of the Less Familiar

How many times have you attended worship at a church that is not of your tradition? Have you worshiped with Baptists, Presbyterians, Pentecostals, Lutherans, Nazarenes, or Episcopalians? It is a marvelous experience. Each of these traditions emphasizes something a little different in their praise and preaching. And each is supported by the Holy Spirit.

It's sad to think that only *our* tradition holds the lock and key to the gates of heaven. You've probably heard the old story about the Pentecostal who, on his first day in heaven, was singing and shouting the glories of God at the top of his voice. St. Peter leaned over and whispered quietly, "Shh. Not so loud. That group over in the corner is our isolationists. We don't want to disturb them because they think they're the only ones here."

Tom explored other traditions. After he spent years worshiping with Baptists, Pentecostals, and the newer, seeker-sensitive churches, Tom and his wife found a home in the more liturgical environment of the Episcopal Church. He found a local parish that supported his more conservative theology but celebrated worship in a way Tom could resonate with more easily.

Attending other church services isn't the only way to explore the land of the less familiar. In fact, it's probably not even the best way. I strongly recommend reading authors who come from a different Christian perspective. Coming from a Baptist seminary and a contemporary evangelical church, I first encountered a new voice with Eugene Peterson, a Presbyterian. I couldn't read enough. A man deeply committed to finding God in our everyday lives, Peterson touched my soul because he used a language that was just a bit different than my tradition. Frederick Buechner, Henri Nouwen, Lesslie Newbigin, Os Guinness, Richard Foster, and Alan Jones all speak of the same gospel, only in excitingly different ways.

Exploring the land of the less familiar helps us see God in fresh ways. We discover anew how big, how complex, and how magnificent a God we serve.

Two: They Are Attentive to God

In *Working the Angles*, Eugene Peterson writes about churches: "The biblical fact is that there are no successful churches. There are instead, communities of sinners, gathered before God week after week in towns and villages all over the world.... In these communities of sinners, one of the sinners is called pastor and given a designated responsibility in the community. The pastor's responsibility is to keep the community attentive to God."

Attentive to God. Those are the operative words. I fear that sometimes, under the influence of a "Too Agreeable God" philosophy, we may expend too much energy trying to make God attentive to us. The irony is, he already is attentive to us by his very nature. We can't "make" him any more attentive.

Instead, the person reinventing a life with God will begin with Peterson's words and focus on being attentive to God. It's another of those backward principles. You can't make God attentive to you, and yet he already is. But by focusing your attention on *him*, you seem to acquire a new set of eyes, ones that see the work he's doing in and around you.

I read of a bishop who instructed his pupils that they were to conduct the church service in exactly the same way no matter the size of the congregation, whether two or two thousand. He then reminded them, "Remember, a worship service is not for the people attending; it is for God! So it makes no difference who or how many are attending."

When I think of "attentive to God," I think of Tevia in *The Fiddler on the Roof*. In a sense the entire play (and movie) is one continual prayer. There is probably more dialogue between Tevia and God than any other two people in the play. Tevia's constant attention is on a God who walks with him, talks with him, and intervenes in all his activities.

A life of acknowledging God is a habitual one: habitual church, habitual prayer, habitual praise, habitual requests, habitual silence before God, and habitual listening. It's impossible to outline a formula, but it is possible to nurture a constant attitude that acknowledges the presence of a very real God.

Three: They Are Honest to God

I was told of a pastor who gave great advice to a person new to the faith who felt awkward with prayer. He told her first of all to try praying on her knees; it would remind her of her humility before God. He then said great words, "Next, I don't want you to pray. Instead, I just want you to talk to God — out loud. Whatever is on your mind, talk about it. You might even tell him that you feel kind of silly talking to someone you can't see."

I recall an editorial written several years ago by Philip Yancey after he spent an entire month doing nothing but reading the Bible cover to cover. Upon concluding his effort, he remarked that he was profoundly struck by the personness and personality of God. Our God is truly multidimensional, exciting, passionate, and *honest*. To me it makes sense for us to pray in that same way.

I have a vivid recollection of a long walk with Father Francis, Abbot of St. Andrews Abbey. I remember being able to tell him all of my frailties, weaknesses, and sins largely because I knew he was safe; the monastery was over a hundred miles from my home, and he didn't know anyone I knew. It was so freeing. But the same is even more true of God. He is eminently safer. We can't shock or embarrass or frustrate him with our troubles or weaknesses. And by being honest to God, we open up a whole new realm of vitality in our growing relationship with him.

Four: They Fight for Love

St. Teresa of Avila, known for her life of prayer, writes that in her first several years at the convent she had a terrible time with prayer. She found no joy in it and thought it to be a very frustrating obligation to God. However, she did not give up. Instead, she persevered and wrestled with the temptation to quit. She fought for her intimacy with God. And succeeded. For the past four hundred years, St. Teresa has served as a model for prayer to the whole church.

Tom Thompson had to fight to love God. By the time he was in his midthirties, he recognized a big void in his soul, and with that came two choices: Give up or fight. Tom chose the latter. But it wasn't an easy fight. Like Jacob, Tom held onto the leg of God and said, "I won't let go!" His fight took several years, several churches, several ministers, and a lot of prayers. But today Tom will tell you that his soul rests in the richest soil yet.

Somehow, in our results-oriented, high-producing, fast-acting culture we have come to expect God to respond in kind. But God doesn't seem to have the same timetable we do. Sometimes reinventing your life with God will take time and considerable effort. A great line from the movie *Dead Man Walking* comes when one man says to the nun something like, "It's not so easy for me, sister. You see, I haven't got your faith." She quickly responds, "Are you kidding? Faith is not so easy for me either. It takes work."

BELIEVE IT

In an earlier chapter we talked about passionate people as being true "believers." They have a real reason to live and, if called to, a real reason to die. Such is our belief about God. The reinvented person who carves his or her mark deep in life will do so with God. What we believe about God is the most valuable of all our assets. And so it would benefit us greatly to ever expand and grow our understanding of his infinite magnitude.

There are some who probably wish I would give a clearer idea of what this "expansive" God might look like. However, if I were to do so, I would only offer up yet another box that would get in the way of the very thing I wish to do. But be assured. Scripture is quite clear: Those who seek a magnificent God will find a magnificent God.

In his letter to the Ephesians Paul writes one of the Bible's greatest prayers when he says, "that you...may know the love of Christ which surpasses knowledge" (NASB). Consider the paradox: that you may know something that is unknowable. The love (and person) of God is so vast and so expansive that it is actually unknowable. And yet Paul prays for us to know it. In the next sentence he even goes so far as to say that it is a prayer God will answer "exceeding abundantly."

The bigger your God, the bigger your life.

Right Turns

RECALL THE RIGHT IDEAS

- It's easy to fall prey to having a shrink-wrapped God who is too small, too safe, too agreeable, too impassionate, and too understandable.
- The bigger your God, the bigger your life.
- The size of your God enlarges when you explore the land of the less familiar.
- Our lives are not about keeping God attentive to us, but learning to be attentive to Him. We were created with an innate need to worship.

DECIDE WHAT'S RIGHT FOR YOU

- When someone mentions the name "Jesus," what do you picture in your mind's eye?
- Is your God always a "reasonable" God? When was the last time you were keenly aware of his "dangerous" side?
- What do you believe about God that is different from your official church position?
- Do your feelings of love increase for a multidimensional God with a full personality?

MAKING THE RIGHT MOVES

- Make a list of the five most shocking things about God in the Bible. Now, don't try to defend them. Just acknowledge that He has the right to confound us.

- Read one book this year written by someone from a Christian tradition different from your own.
- Go to a different church and make it an adventure. What was different? What did you like? Learn?
- Pray for eyes to see God as he is. But also remember that you cannot completely pin him down. He is a mystery to be pursued with abandon and passion all of your days.

Our society is obsessed with personal rights, but it will survive
only if we adopt personal obligations.

DENNIS PRAGER
FROM *THINK A SECOND TIME*

"Just as the Son of Man did not come to be served, but to serve,
and to give his life as a ransom for many..."

MATTHEW 20:28

CHAPTER TWELVE

IT'S ALL IN
YOUR AIM

W e began this book by asking, "Could one question change the rest of your life?"

You bet. When John Sculley was asked by Steve Jobs whether he wanted "to spend the rest of his life selling sugared water or take a chance to change the world," his life was altered forever.

What question (or questions) might *continually* change the rest of your life forever? For me, there are two — which I would guess are the same for you.

1. What are your right things?
2. What are you doing today to get them right?

Of all our daily demands, activities, and encounters, only four things rise above the others as ones we need to get right. We've called them the Four Ps: passion, purpose, people, and praise.

Passion considers how you approach life. Is it with curiosity and fervor, or with dread and dismay? *Purpose* is all about accomplishing something significant for yourself and others around you. *People* is about how you pursue and maintain important relationships. And finally, *Praise* recognizes there is someone in the universe even greater than our passion, purpose, and people. He gives eternal meaning to these three, since all of them exist in his image. Praise is about loving, following, and being attentive to God.

In addition to the Four Ps, we've discussed strategies and tools to help you get the right things right...

1. An understanding of what you "must do" in light of your assets, liabilities, and value

2. A "dream" or vision of who you want to be and a plan to get started

3. A "stable" foundation from which to initiate exciting changes

4. A willingness and methodology for taking "calculated risks"

5. A cadre of great relationships that you support "strategically"

6. A habit of creating "extreme dignity" everywhere you go

We are left with one final question. After we get some of these right things right, what do we do next? What are we really aiming for? Certainly we're not after a "together" life we can show off. Nor are we merely after personal gratification or a false sense of control. We're aiming for a life that matters to a lot more people than just ourselves. Here are three things which, even if only *aimed* at, will keep your life on target in the years to come.

AIM #1
AIM TO GIVE IT AWAY

This is our ultimate goal: Jesus said if you want to save your life, you're gonna have to lose it. The reinvented life will never succeed if the motivation is purely self-centered. It has to go beyond the "I" questions such as, "How can *I* be happiest?" "How can *I* get more and be more?"

The true aim of our lives, the number one reason to get the right things right, is so we can give the right kind of life away to others. Remember in chapter one the corporate staffers who wanted to help kids, to do something good? They wanted a life of significance, a life that matters — not just to them, *but to others*. A reinvented life is about making an impact somewhere.

Even a brief examination of the Four Ps shows that "giving" is the prime directive: You give your *passionate approach* to those around you; your most favored *accomplishments* are those which result in the satisfaction and well-being of others; the sole motivation of your *love* is to help fill that lonely hole in the rest of us; and the objective of your *praise* is to give back to God.

The reinvented giver is an odd commodity. He is odd, first of all, because he gives from a position of strength. His giving originates from his most valuable assets, while consciously avoiding a "wrong rule" type giving. Secondly, he is even odder because his life is marked by his attitude of care for others. He gives time, attention, and dignity to the needs of those around him.

Without exception, the world's most respected people are the givers. Jimmy Carter will be remembered for decades for his legacy of gifts to the human race more than for his power as a president. Mother Teresa, who may be the most widely known and respected name across international borders, is revered for her self-sacrifice to her God and to the poor. And on a more common level, Dave Appleton, a project manager in Saudi Arabia, is known for his engineering expertise, but admired for his unwavering commitment and service to the people around him.

You get what you want most only when you give it away.

Here is a basic truth: You were created to give. And not only that, you were created to receive from giving. It's another backward, "unreasonable" idea.

And what you receive is far more important than anything material. You receive a filling of your spirit, of your soul, of the deepest, most valuable parts within you. It is the fulfillment of your ultimate call — the call to love and serve God and people.

Giving as the Route to Self-Esteem

In the last twenty years we have been exposed to an ideology which claims the best route to personal fulfillment is through improving your self-esteem. So much emphasis has been placed on the value of self-esteem that we have been led to believe that our ultimate goal in life is to acquire a healthy self-image.

The irony is that the most surefire way to have a low self-esteem is to pursue a high one. Paul Vitz, professor of psychology at New York University, claims in his book *Psychology as Religion* that if you try to acquire self-esteem, you will surely fail. Numerous studies support the thesis. The only way for you to validate yourself is by what you do, not by who you claim to be. Dr. Vitz summarizes the issues clearly and succinctly: "Try to acquire self-esteem and you will fail — but do good to others and accomplish something for yourself, and you will have all the self-esteem you need."

Self-esteem is really an issue concerning personal value and begs the question, "What am I worth?" According to Vitz (and verified by the Bible), you will never be worth more than when you give away what you have — your talents and your love.

Giving as the Route to Opportunity

In a way I hate to suggest that by giving more you get more, as if it somehow spoils a purely altruistic heart. And yet, it is true.

I learned an important lesson in 1980. As I had just entered the Christian faith, I expressed an interest in serving the church in some capacity. Not too long afterwards I was approached by a high-level volunteer and asked if I would be interested in being a chairman. I was quite proud that they had already taken note of my leadership skills — until I discovered that they literally meant "chair" man. He wanted to know if I would join the volunteer crew assigned to moving the two thousand chairs necessary to set up each Sunday.

It was, for me, a wonderful growth opportunity. I got to know a bunch of guys in the church, guys who were willing to sweat and receive little glory. Oddly enough, however, of the dozen or so regularly committed "chair" men, three went on to be elders, one became the church administrator, and one received a seminary education and returned to be a staff pastor of this twelve-thousand-member church.

"Giving yourself away" is simply another of those backward principles: You get what you want most only when you give it away.

I was on the road one night in Calgary, Alberta, when I caught a television special about basketball-great George "The Ice Man" Gervin, who now spends his time helping men improve themselves. Of his work Gervin said, "It is one man's doin' to help another man become a better man." He said it all.

AIM #2

AIM TO CONTINUE

Now here's a thought: In reality, there's no such thing as a "reinvented life." That's because life is always in process, and we never stop growing. Therefore, in a very real sense, we are always reinventing. The person who is trying to *get* the right things right will probably never succeed if he thinks he will discover some final destination here on this planet. Instead, the people who are *getting* the right things right will always be in that process, checking their lives, their motives, their actions. So how does one succeed at staying on track and not going back to the old ways?

Keep a Constant Black-Hole Watch

Remember the black holes discussed early on — busyness, stuckness, and hopelessness? They, as well as a host of others, find a way of gradually creeping their way back into our lives. "Busyness" does not occur overnight, nor does stuckness or hopelessness. As sneaky and insidious little culprits, they can be on us before we see them coming.

So don't be surprised when you discover a black hole. The difference now is you have a few more tools in the toolbox to resist them. (See the matrix on pages 231-232 for more ideas.)

Regularly Review Your Goals

As stated in an earlier chapter, I believe the primary reason corporations and individuals don't succeed is not that they fail to dream and plan, but that they *fail to measure*. All you have to do is review your annual goals one time each quarter (one to two hours per year!) to keep you on the reinventing track.

Review and Modify Your Vision

Just because we created a vision doesn't mean it's there for life. We are in a constant state of repair as we change our lives and God changes us. I find incredible fun and mystery in the prospect of continued reinvention. For some people, reinvention requires only minor tweaking. For others, there may be major overhauls.

But no matter how drastic the changes *the right things always remain the same*. The successful life will always focus on passion, purpose, people, and praise.

Give Yourself Lots of Grace

Most of us have a hard time with the idea of falling back to where we started. We believe that we are somehow less of a person if we start a plan and two months later fail to see great improvement. And as a result, we just give up. When the idea of a life that matters becomes something too hard to do, or too rigid, we stop. When it no longer holds excitement and adventure, we will lose the passion to proceed.

My hope is that all of us would learn to give ourselves permission to fail more. We must give more than lip service to the fact that we are imperfect people on an imperfect planet. We all have high hopes that rarely turn out exactly the way we planned. But the fun comes in the trying. If we fail or proceed more slowly than we might have wished, so what? We learn and get better. The reinvented life is dying all the time, to be resurrected again with fresh life and goodwill.

AIM #3

AIM TO INTERWEAVE

We in the Western world love to compartmentalize. We break things down into their logical components in an effort to analyze and evaluate. You find evidence of it everywhere. Businesses have their "five critical success factors," governments have their "four-pronged approach," preachers have their "three-point sermons," and even I suggest the "Four Ps."

I know a major company that decided the best way to organize their business was to divide into several "business units," each with a mandate to manage their piece of the corporate pie as if it were a separate entity. These business units were allocated a specific measure of corporate resources and were also given direct accountability for their own profits and losses. By decentralizing, the theory went, each group could better manage its business. It was a great idea — on paper.

The only problem was it didn't work. They soon discovered the value of greater integration. No one had anticipated the need for the mutual sharing of resources. For example, suppose groups A and B are each given one million dollars to develop new projects. That's good until you find out that group A has discovered an opportunity for tremendous growth, while group B has no new discoveries. In order to proceed, group A needs some of group B's resources. But since group B is being measured strictly on its own successes, why should it give away its resources? There is no incentive.

The company now maintains a more integrated approach. While it still uses the business unit framework, it has created systems to handle the overlap and fuzziness that comes with normal production life in a large company. They have created a system that acknowledges that value of managing the pieces without compromising the success of the whole.

The same principle holds true with the Four Ps. Breaking down our lives into only four key areas is extraordinarily helpful. It creates focus and offers a framework for clarity. However, the best way to actualize the Four Ps is to integrate them in a system so it becomes difficult to tell where the passion leaves off and the purpose begins, or exactly where the praise component enters the picture because we understand that God is fully involved in everything we do.

I like to think of this as going beyond mere integration. It is more like an interweaving where the Four Ps are the primary colored threads we use to sew the warp and woof of our lives. Each colored thread is critical to the final product. It must be exquisitely manufactured on its own, but when it is woven into the final fabric, it becomes so enmeshed with the others that its distinction becomes hardly visible.

In the same way, a real target for your reinvented life is to aim for an "interwovenness" in all your right things. For example, on a Saturday afternoon you're playing ball with your son. You enjoy being outdoors, teaching your boy the pivot for a double play; you love being with him, all the while thanking God for this whole opportunity. That's interwovenness.

But when you find yourself in the same situation thinking of a problem at the office, you lose passion. Or if instead of playing with your son, you decide for the fourth consecutive week to continue repairing those garage shelves, you lose the "people" piece. Or if you forget that this wonderful day is a gift from God, you lose praise. In so many different ways you can relinquish the wonder of an interwoven life.

Take a moment to think back on a "great time period" in your life — a period of six months to three years where you felt life was great. I'd be willing to bet that all four Ps were strongly present: You were excited about life; you had a sense you were going somewhere; you were surrounded by people you loved to be with; and there was a sense of eternal comfort.

Now consider another period of time where things were not as great. Maybe it was a period of major frustration or burnout or busyness or bitterness; possibly it was a time of terrible loss. As you ponder this difficult period, which of the Four Ps were most noticeably absent? It could be that work was going well but you felt a "hole in your soul" and sensed a need for God, or you weren't spending enough time with your husband, or you had failed to take care of your "fun side."

Each of the Ps has a domino effect on the others. When one is strong, it builds up the others; but conversely, when one is weak, it drains your whole life. They are truly interwoven. So, if you experience a pitfall, you might think about an interwoven approach as a remedy. Consider the following matrix.

ISSUE	POSSIBLE PROBLEMS	POSSIBLE SOLUTIONS
HOPELESSNESS	Loss of passion Small God Stuck in the "stable" Lack of vision	Do what you love Expand your view Take calculated risks Create your vision
STUCKNESS	No plan for success Fear of change Unable to see a bright future	PDCA Take calculated risks Dreamstarts

ISSUE	POSSIBLE PROBLEMS	POSSIBLE SOLUTIONS
BURNOUT	Loss of passion	Do what you love
	Few tangible accom-plishments	Create/follow goals list
	No real friends	Strategic love
	Small God	Stable change
BUSYNESS	Too many people	Draining/Neutral/Replenishing
	Too much work	*Make* time for passion/people
	Too many demands	Create/follow goals list
FRUSTRATION	Few tangible accomplishments	Create/follow goals list
	Lack of vision	Create your vision
	Others running your life	Avoid wrong rules/know self
	Stuck in the "stable"	Calculated risks

The Interwoven Ps are a natural phenomenon. Life, all on its own, has a way of integrating and interweaving. The only time we need to take it apart is for analysis, improvement, and repair. After we improve or repair the item in question, we simply sit back and let it all work naturally.

MANAGING THE PARADOX

We've come a long way, you and I. I've attempted to offer a fresh perspective for hope, for change, and for personal significance. There are, indeed, a lot of things you will do in your lifetime, and a few of them will be really right ones. My hope is that those are the ones you do really right.

But I have a concern. I am concerned that after reading a book like this, with its success stories of people who reinvented the life they wanted, you may be motivated to act — but then you will forget. You will forget that along with the joys of self-reinvention (and they are multifarious) come also the pain and the boredom and the despondence and the everyday difficulties of life on a broken planet.

Getting the right things right will make a huge difference in your life. I've seen it work many times. But it is not a panacea. Life is still difficult.

Consider some of the successful reinventors mentioned throughout the book: Denny, Jack, and Matt. Each of them continues to face the difficult task of life. Denny Bellesi, who built a large church from scratch, has to wage the daily budget battles that are common in a church that grows quickly. There are even days he wonders why he is doing it at all. Although Jack Burns founded a successful company, he spent most of his life alone, wrestling with the pain of being single and not finding a wife. It was not until his early forties that he married for the first time. Matt continues to face the ongoing issues of a divorce and noncustodial parenthood.

Life is a paradox of difficult and unpredictable wonder. Denny, Jack, Matt, and a host of other brave and simple people like them have successfully reinvented themselves by learning to manage the paradox. They did it through perseverance, desire, and hard work.

And they did it knowing they were not alone. They had support. They had friends, and they had internal drive.

But, most of all, they had God.

Unless the LORD builds the house,
its builders labor in vain.
Unless the LORD watches over the city,
the watchmen stand guard in vain.

You can rest your reinvented life on God, the ultimate reinventor, the resurrector of renewed and impassioned living. Passion, purpose, people, and praise are all aligned with the designs of the Creator.

The life you want is before you now. It just begins with a beginning. In the end there are only a few things you will need to do right...

Right Turns

RECALL THE RIGHT IDEAS

- Two questions can continually change the rest of a person's life: 1. What are my right things? 2. What am I doing today to get them right?
- What we are aiming at is as important as what we accomplish. We're not merely after personal gratification or a false sense of control. We're aiming at a life that matters to a lot more people than just ourselves.

- Three things, even if only aimed at, will keep our lives on target: to give our lives away, to continue to grow, to integrate the four Ps.
- We will never finish reinventing our lives. It is a journey — a way of living — not a destination.

DECIDE WHAT'S RIGHT FOR YOU

- What is the biggest personal change you've made as a result of reading this book?
- Have you begun to reinvent the life you really want? Have you gotten closer to knowing what that looks like?
- When is it often hard for you to integrate the four Ps into your life?
- Consider the stories of Matt, Jack, and Denny. Are you prepared for a hard but wonderful life?

MAKE THE RIGHT MOVES

- List the elements of the life you *thought* you wanted when you started this book. Now list the elements of the life you really want *and* were created to have. What are the differences?
- Think of two specific ways to aim for the three targets listed here: to give, to continue, to integrate.
- Take a walk today, even if it's only one block, and with every step think about what is truly important to you.
- When you are done, take time to fix your eyes on God, the Author and only true Inventor of life, without whom all your efforts will fall short.

Notes

Introduction

Max DePree, *Leadership Is an Art* (New York: Bantam Doubleday Dell Publishing Group Inc., 1990), 17–19.

John Sculley, *Odyssey* (New York: Harper & Row, Publishers, 1987), 90.

Chapter One

Michael Crichton, *The Lost World* (New York: Alfred A. Knopf, 1995), 4.

Charles Handy, *The Age of Unreason* (Boston: Harvard Business School Press, 1990).

Chapter Two

William F. Arndt and F. Wilbur Gingrich, *A Greek-English Lexicon of the New Testament and Other Early Christian Literature* (Chicago: The University of Chicago Press), s.v. "splanknon," 763.

Peter Drucker, *The Effective Executive* (New York: HarperCollins Publishers, Inc.), 1.

Blaise Pascal, *Pensées* (Harmondsworth, Middlesex, England: Penguin Books, Ltd., 1966).

Chapter Three

Robert Farrar Capon, *Between Noon and Three: A Parable of Romance, Law and the Outrage of Grace* (San Francisco: Harper & Row, Publishers, 1982), 148.

M. Scott Peck, *The Road Less Traveled* (New York: Simon and Schuster, 1978), 15.

Chapter Four

Alan Jones, *Journey into Christ* (San Francisco: Harper & Row, Publishers, 1977), 91–92.

Basil Pennington, *Daily We Follow Him* (n.p., n.d.).

Chapter Five

Isabel Briggs Myers with Peter B. Myers, *Gifts Differing* (Palo Alto, Calif.: Consulting Psychologists Press, 1980).

Frederick Buechner, *Telling the Truth: The Gospel as Tragedy, Comedy and*

Fairy Tale (San Francisco: Harper & Row, Publishers, 1977).

David DuPree, "Jordan: Security before big money," *USA Today,* n.d.

Thomas A. Harris, *I'm Okay, You're Okay* (New York: Harper & Row, Publishers, 1967, 1968, 1969).

Ranier Maria Rilke, *Letters to a Young Poet,* trans. M. D. Herter Norton (New York: W. W. Norton & Company, 1934), 18–19.

James Bryan Smith, *Embracing the Love of God* (San Francisco: Harper San Francisco, 1995), 3.

St. Teresa of Avila, *A Life of Prayer,* ed. James M. Houston (Portland, Ore.: Multnomah Press, 1983).

Chapter Seven

Isabel Briggs Myers with Peter B. Myers, *Gifts Differing* (Palo Alto, Calif.: Consulting Psychologists Press, 1980).

A Shorter Morning and Evening Prayer: The Psalter of the Divine Office (Great Britain: The Chaucer Press, Richard Clay Ltd, 1983).

Neil Postman, *The Disappearance of Childhood* (New York: Vintage Books, 1982, 1994).

Marsha Sinetar, *Do What You Love, the Money Will Follow* (New York: Paulist Press, 1987).

David Wilcox, *All the Roots Grow Deeper* (Big Horizon CD).

Chapter Eight

Gustav Berle, "Letters," *INC.,* May 1992, 17.

Stephen R. Covey, *The 7 Habits of Highly Effective People* (New York: Simon & Schuster, Inc. 1989), 67–94.

Kevin Maney, "Former Silicon Valley brat hits his stride," *USA Today,* November 1995.

Kweisi Mfume, "Interview" *U.S. News & World Report,* 25 December 1995, 62.

Tom Peters, *Thriving on Chaos* (New York: Alfred A. Knopf, 1987).

David Whyte, *The Heart Aroused* (New York: Doubleday, 1994), 71.

Chapter Nine

Robert N. Bellah et al., *Habits of the Heart* (San Francisco: Harper & Row, Publishers, 1985), 115.

St. Teresa of Avila, *A Life of Prayer,* ed. James M. Houston (Portland, Ore.: Multnomah Press, 1983).

Chapter Ten
C. S. Lewis, *Perelandra* (New York: Collier Books, 1944), 205.
Wes Roberts, *Leadership Secrets of Attila the Hun* (New York: Warner Books, Inc., 1989), 109.

Chapter Eleven
C. S. Lewis, *The Lion, the Witch and the Wardrobe* (New York: Collier Books, 1950), 75–76.
Eugene Peterson, *Working the Angles: The Shape of Pastoral Integrity* (Grand Rapids: William B. Eerdmans Publishing Company, 1987), 2.
St. Teresa of Avila, *A Life of Prayer,* ed. James M. Houston (Portland, Ore.: Multnomah Press, 1983), 1–23.
Elie Wiesel, *Souls on Fire,* trans. Marion Wiesel (New York: Summit Books, 1972), 45, 49, 83–84.

Chapter Twelve
Dennis Prager, *Think a Second Time* (New York: HarperCollins Publishers, 1995), 15.
Paul C. Vitz, *Psychology as Religion* (Grand Rapids: William B. Eerdmans Publishing Company, 1977, 1994), 19.

For information regarding personal development,
management consulting or seminars/conferences,
please contact:
Hedges & Associates
P.O. Box 4828
Mission Viejo, CA 92690-4828
Fax 714-348-2732
CompuServe 73642,2453